YORK NOTES

General Editors: Professor A.N. J
of Stirling) & Professor Suheil Bus.... ....
University of Beirut)

Charles Dickens

DAVID COPPERFIELD

Notes by R.W. Stevenson

MA (EDINBURGH) M LITT (OXFORD)
Lecturer in English Literature,
University of Edinburgh

LONGMAN
YORK PRESS

YORK PRESS
Immeuble Esseily, Place Riad Solh, Beirut

LONGMAN GROUP UK LIMITED
Longman House, Burnt Mill, Harlow,
Essex CM20 2JE, England
Associated companies, branches and representatives
throughout the world

First published 1980
Sixth impression 1993

ISBN 0-582-78131-0

Produced by Longman Singapore Publishers Pte Ltd
Printed in Singapore

Contents

Part 1

Introduction

EVER SINCE the publication of *Pickwick Papers* (1836–7), Charles Dickens has occupied a special place in the hearts and minds of his many readers. During his own lifetime, Dickens was appreciated not only by the mass of the British public, but even by Queen Victoria herself, and his popularity has remained very high ever since. His novels have always been best-sellers, and are frequently adapted for film, television, and the theatre. He created a fictional world imagined with peculiarly memorable vitality, and familiarity with his work and his characters is so vivid and universal that the adjective 'Dickensian' has become part of the English language. Dickens's work has become a permanent part of the thought and outlook of English-speaking people. His uniquely entertaining novels are a continuing popular success, and he has also come to be increasingly respected by literary critics as a powerful and original artist.

David Copperfield has always been one of Dickens's most popular works, and many critics think it is his best. Dickens said himself that it was his favourite of his own novels: in his preface to the 1869 edition, he remarked:

'Of all my books, I like this the best. It will be easily believed that I am a fond parent to every child of my fancy ... But, like many fond parents, I have in my heart of hearts a favourite child. And his name is DAVID COPPERFIELD.'

Perhaps Dickens was especially fond of *David Copperfield* because David's story is often very close to the history of his own life. Dickens commented in 1850 'I do not find it easy to get sufficiently far away from this Book', and talked of 'personal confidences, and private emotions' in it. In studying a work of literature, it is always interesting and often useful to learn something about its author, and this is especially true of *David Copperfield*. A comparison of its story with Dickens's own life reveals the similarity of many episodes and may partly suggest how Dickens came to write the novel as he did. So we begin with a short biography of Charles Dickens, concentrating on his life up to the publication of *David Copperfield* in 1849–50.

The life of Charles Dickens (1812–70)

On 7 February 1812, Charles Dickens was born at Portsea, near Portsmouth, on the south coast of England. He was the second of eight children in the family of John Dickens, who worked as a clerk for the Navy. Charles later remarked 'I know my father to be as kind-hearted and generous a man as ever lived in the world'*. John Dickens does seem to have been a warm and pleasant father, but his lack of responsibility, especially with money, later led his family into serious difficulties. Charles's early childhood, however, was happy. When he was two years old, the family moved briefly to London, and then to Chatham, a naval base thirty miles south-east of London. Charles attended school there until he was nine, and, as a small boy who did not greatly enjoy games, he spent a lot of time reading.

In 1822, less pleasant times began. The family moved to London, and, as they were now very short of money, Charles was no longer sent to school. Worse than that, despite his efforts to save money by selling and pawning household goods, John Dickens was arrested for debt and taken to the Marshalsea prison. He was later joined there by the rest of his family, except Charles: to help his family's finances, he had been sent to work in a blacking factory. His job was wrapping and labelling bottles of blacking (a kind of shoe polish) for a wage of six shillings a week.

These events had an enormous effect on Charles Dickens. He was very deeply affected by the double shock of the shame and misery of his family, and his own disgust and loneliness in the factory. He was forced to work for twelve hours a day in unpleasant surroundings, returning at night to his solitary room, earning only just enough to buy food, and often wandering alone around London. He was a sensitive and intelligent boy, only twelve years old, and his position was miserable enough in itself. But it was made worse by Charles feeling so humiliated by it, and bitterly thinking he had lost all chance of progress in life. Dickens later remarked of this part of his childhood 'How much I suffered, it is ... utterly beyond my power to tell ... No words can express the secret agony of my soul'†. He could never forget this period of lonely hopelessness, although its recollection was so painful to him that he almost never mentioned it even to his closest friends. Lost, lonely, orphaned, or badly-treated children very often appear in Dickens's novels. (Think how many orphans, or children with only one parent, there are in *David Copperfield*). The sympathy and compassionate imagination with which Dickens wrote about such children may have come partly from memories of his own unhappiness when young.

*John Forster, *The Life of Charles Dickens*, ed. J.W.T. Ley, p.10.
†Forster, *The Life of Charles Dickens*, p.26, p.29.

Although John Dickens was released from prison after three months, it was some time before he took his son from the factory and sent him to Wellington House, a school run by a harsh headmaster. Charles remained for two years, and did well, although his father later remarked of him 'He may be said to have educated himself'*. After leaving school at the age of fifteen, Dickens became a clerk in a lawyers' office. Deciding to become a parliamentary reporter, he taught himself short-hand, with great determination, while continuing to work in the office. He also began reading seriously and widely in London libraries. At this time, he became very familiar with London and its life. In particular, he developed a great love for the theatre. This interest continued throughout his life and was later reflected in his novels.

When Dickens was eighteen, he fell passionately in love with Maria Beadnell, a pretty, careless girl. She was the daughter of a bank manager, and her family did not like Dickens's poverty, or his lack of prospects. She herself seems to have treated him rather coldly. The affair lasted for several years, eventually came to nothing, and was a most unhappy one for Dickens. Like the blacking factory episode, memories of his desperate intensity at this time remained with him long afterwards.

Nevertheless, Dickens's determination to succeed continued, and in 1832 he became a parliamentary reporter, as he had wished. He also wrote some short pieces for magazines, under the pen-name 'Boz'. A popular volume of these, *Sketches by Boz*, Dickens's first book, appeared on his twenty-fourth birthday. In 1836, he began writing an amusing monthly serial, *Pickwick Papers*, which became extremely popular and brought him both wealth and an immediate fame which lasted through-out his life. *Pickwick Papers* was read everywhere, and Charles Dickens became a celebrated name. Shortly after *Pickwick Papers* began to appear, in April 1836, Dickens was married to Catherine Hogarth, the daughter of a fellow journalist. Although they were together for twenty-two years and had ten children, Catherine was not an ideal companion, and the marriage does not seem to have been entirely happy. Dickens's constant energy made him restless, and he left Catherine in 1858. He later befriended a young actress, Ellen Ternan.

After *Pickwick Papers*, Dickens continued his popular success with more novels: *Oliver Twist* (1837), *Nicholas Nickleby* (1838), *The Old Curiosity Shop* (1840–1), and *Barnaby Rudge* (1841). He toured America, and travelled widely in Europe, publishing two more novels before *David Copperfield* appeared in 1849–50, partly reflecting his own experiences up to that date.

Charles Dickens led an extremely busy life. After *David Copperfield*, he published six more novels, and was at work on a seventh when he

*Forster, *The Life of Charles Dickens*, p.47.

died in June 1870. As well as novels, Dickens was very active in writing for newspapers, supporting his extensive interest in public affairs and social questions. This interest was not confined to writing: Dickens was involved in many charities and helped both with personal advice and large gifts of money. In addition to this charity work, and his demanding social life as a famous and successful public figure, Dickens enjoyed using his brilliant talent for acting. First he performed in various plays, in which he often took the leading part, and later, starting in 1858, in public readings from his own works. Although he was a very energetic man, his involvement in so many activities was exhausting, and the public readings particularly wore him down. He died after collapsing during one of these performances, at the age of fifty-eight. He was deeply mourned by his huge public. He is buried in Westminster Abbey.

What similarities do you notice between the lives of David Copperfield and Charles Dickens? There are several comparable episodes, particularly in their youthful experiences. Like Dickens, David Copperfield was forced to work miserably in a warehouse when a boy; led a similar life in London; went to a school rather like Dickens's own; worked for a time in a lawyers' office; taught himself shorthand and became a parliamentary reporter; fell passionately in love at an early age; and later became a successful novelist. In a letter he wrote to Maria Beadnell many years after their affair was over, Dickens admitted that he had used his memories of it in creating the character of Dora, and in describing David Copperfield's love for her. Dickens also seems to have put some of his memories of his father into the character of Mr Micawber. Like Micawber, John Dickens was quite unable to look after money: he is also said to have talked and written letters in the same grand and impressive way that Micawber uses, and his arrest for debt is like Micawber's brief period in the King's Bench prison.

Dickens once actually began to write an autobiography, but gave this up and wrote *David Copperfield* instead. It is clear that he uses *David Copperfield* as a way of looking back over his own life. Many of his own experiences appear in the novel. From a comparison of the two stories we can learn a lot about Dickens himself, and about his creative act in writing David Copperfield as a fictionalised autobiography.

Of course, David Copperfield is not Charles Dickens, nor is *David Copperfield* precisely the story of Dickens's own life. After all, David's affair with Dora, for example, ends happily in marriage, while Dickens's affair with Maria Beadnell ended very unhappily. Considering Dickens's life alongside David's is an interesting comparison, but should not lead us to suppose an exact correspondence. All authors use their own experience in their writing: *David Copperfield* is unusual only because it seems to copy some of the events of Charles Dickens's life so very closely.

Dickens and the Victorian era

When *David Copperfield* first appeared in 1850, life in Britain was very different from what it is nowadays. Society was still much more strictly divided into rich and poor, and ladies and gentlemen were treated very differently from the working classes. In *David Copperfield*, notice, for example, how proudly Mrs Steerforth treats Mr Peggotty. Religious faith was firmer than it is today, and sometimes took quite a severe form, as in the Murdstones' 'austere and wrathful' religion.

Most of Charles Dickens's active life was spent during the reign of Queen Victoria (1837–1901). The Victorian era is often thought of as a time of prosperity, stability, and a successful British power which created a huge empire by the end of the nineteenth century. But this was also a time of great change and disturbance: it was during the Victorian period, and particularly in the years 1840–80, that modern Britain developed and evolved. Britain's wealth was based on the profits from the Industrial Revolution in the late eighteenth and early nine-teenth centuries, which introduced machine production and made the factory the centre of work. In an expanding economic situation, the population also grew rapidly (it doubled between 1800 and 1850), and centred increasingly on life in towns and cities which grew up around the factories. The old, slower, country ways of life declined, especially after the development of railways around 1840.

The growth of cities created many social problems: poor housing, crime, bad sanitation, poor education, disease, poverty, and so on. Prostitution, for example, was very widespread in London in the eighteen-fifties. Although the Victorian period is often thought of as a time of Britain's greatness, daily life in the mid-nineteenth century was often hard for large sections of the city population. Wages were low, families large, and housing often overcrowded. Even women and children (like David Copperfield, or Dickens himself) were forced to work in factories, often for twelve hours or more every day.

Some political changes of the period, however, allowed hope that problems would be overcome by government action. The Great Reform Act of 1832, by allowing more people to vote, considerably altered Parliament around the time when Dickens began his work there as a reporter.

Dickens was always deeply concerned with the social problems of his time. This can be seen in his journalism and charitable works, as well as in his novels. Part of the reason for Dickens's popularity was that he was seriously and compassionately interested in the welfare of the mass of the people, and determined to attack any social evil which made their lives unhappy. As a result, many of his novels are at least partly concerned with social issues. This is perhaps less true of *David Cop-*

perfield than of some other works, but even here we can see that Dickens wanted to make his readers think about several of the social problems of their time. The question of education is taken up in describing Mr Murdstone's cruel attempt to frighten David into learning (Chapter 4), and in the contrast between Creakle's miserable and ineffective school, where the pupils are beaten and badly taught (Chapter 7), and Doctor Strong's, 'as different from Mr Creakle's as good is from evil' (Chapter 16). Later, Creakle turns up again as a prison superintendent (Chapter 61). Dickens included this chapter in order to give his opinion about the topical question of prison organisation. The problem of prostitution is tactfully considered in the story of Martha Endell. Dickens himself was involved with a charity which helped and cared for such women. He was also interested in the possible benefits of emigration, and the success of Mr Micawber and Mr Peggotty in Australia, at the end of the novel, can be taken as an advertisement for the possibility of a better life in a new land. Another example of a contemporary issue in *David Copperfield* is the severe criticism of Doctors' Commons (Chapters 23, 26, 33, 39) as an out-of-date and inefficient legal institution. Perhaps Mr Micawber's arrest for debt is meant to show the harshness of the law, but his cheerful optimism almost turns the episode into a holiday.

More generally, a great strength of Dickens's awareness of his contemporary history is his sensitivity to the spreading city landscapes of the Victorian era, particularly of London. There is an intense energy in his descriptions of them. For example, there are the scenes of David's wanderings while he is working at the warehouse (Chapter 11), or of Martha among the rubbish of the riverside (Chapter 47).

Dickens had suffered in his early life, and never forgot what this meant, for himself and for others. His sympathetic awareness of contemporary social problems, and of the lives of the poor, the sick, and the unfortunate, is a constant feature of his work.

Setting

David Copperfield is set in five main locations: Blunderstone, Yarmouth, London, Dover and Canterbury. From the many descriptions of travel between these places by stage coach, we know that the action of the novel takes place before the spread of railways, and probably slightly before the Victorian period began. Most of the scenes are set in or around London, and there is a strong sense of the city throughout.

Literary background and other influences

Dickens had a very original mind, and it is not worth spending too much time looking for literary influences on his technique as a novelist. However, consider this passage where David Copperfield recalls his childhood reading in Blunderstone Rookery:

> My father had left a small collection of books in a little room upstairs, to which I had access (for it adjoined my own) and which nobody else in our house ever troubled. From that blessed little room, Roderick Random, Peregrine Pickle, Humphrey Clinker, Tom Jones, The Vicar of Wakefield, Don Quixote, Gil Blas, and Robinson Crusoe, came out, a glorious host, to keep me company. They kept alive my fancy, and my hope of something beyond that place and time,—they, and the *Arabian Nights*, and the *Tales of the Genii*. (Chapter 4).

Dickens's biographer Forster tells us that Dickens's own childhood reading was exactly the same as David's. Perhaps in some ways Dickens followed Smollett, the author of *Roderick Random* (1748), and *Peregrine Pickle* (1751) and *Humphrey Clinker* (1771), and Fielding, the author of *Tom Jones* (1749). Like them, he wrote novels, like *David Copperfield*, which tell the story of someone's life from birth onwards. Like them, he was more interested in showing the nature of character than he was in creating a convincing plot. Dickens's liking for the *Arabian Nights* and *Tales of the Genii*, both collections of fabulous and incredible stories, perhaps accounts for the fantastic and energetic nature of his own imagination. He was also very familiar with Shakespeare, and quotations from the plays and references to them often occur in his novels. Mr Micawber, for example, is very fond of quoting from Shakespeare.

Although he was very well read, two of the main influences on Dickens's style came not from books but from his own experience. Firstly, his training and practice as a journalist taught him accurate description and concern with detail, and gave him a talent for presenting a scene briefly but clearly. Secondly, as a young man Dickens attended the theatre almost every evening, and later acted frequently himself. The theatre may have taught him the use of the comic, and the importance of dialogue: there is an unusual amount of direct speech in Dickens's novels. The theatre perhaps also helped Dickens to learn his 'dramatic' style of presenting action vividly and visually.

A note on the text

Pickwick Papers was a monthly serial, and Dickens followed with all his later novels this successful method of publication. *David Copperfield* first appeared in twenty monthly parts, from May 1849 to November 1850, with illustrations by 'Phiz' (Hablôt K. Browne). A single-volume edition of *David Copperfield* was published in 1850, with a preface by Dickens. The Cheap Edition followed in 1858. The 'Charles Dickens' edition appeared in 1869, with a new preface by Dickens.

There are very many modern editions of *David Copperfield*. Perhaps the best of these for students, especially those for whom English is a second language, is the Longmans edition, London, 1964. This has a useful introduction and thorough explanatory notes. However, the Penguin edition, Harmondsworth, 1966, is cheap, has a good introduction, and reproduces several of the original illustrations. The 'Oxford Illustrated Dickens', London, 1947, includes all these pictures, which are worth looking at. Dickens always made sure that his scenes were drawn exactly as he wanted them to be shown. Two other cheap editions are the Signet, New York, 1962, and the Pan edition, London, 1967. The latter has a good introduction, some notes and several of the illustrations.

Part 2

Summaries

of DAVID COPPERFIELD

A general summary

David Copperfield is David's narration in his maturity of the events and incidents through which he remembers his life and character developing, and through which his maturity was reached.

Six months before David Copperfield's birth, his father died. His aunt, Betsey Trotwood, arrives in Blunderstone on the night he is born, but immediately gives up all interest in him, as she had firmly expected a girl. With his gentle mother Clara Copperfield and his beloved nurse Peggotty, David's early childhood is very happy. Peggotty takes him on holiday to Yarmouth, where they stay in an old boat-house with her brother Mr Peggotty, his nephew Ham and pretty niece little Em'ly, and the forlorn widow Mrs Gummidge. David's happiness ends when he returns home to find his mother has re-married. Her new husband, Murdstone, and his sister Jane, drive Clara to an early grave with their cruel 'firmness'.

David is sent away to Salem House, a school run by a harsh, cruel headmaster, Creakle. He makes two friends there: the apparently charming Steerforth and the agreeable Traddles. But after his mother's death, he is sent instead to work in Murdstone's London warehouse, where he miserably experiences poverty, despair, and loneliness. He lodges with the family of the extraordinary Mr Micawber, whose continual financial difficulties lead to his eventual imprisonment for debt.

David decides to run away to his Aunt Betsey in Dover. Penniless and alone, he has to walk all the way. He finds her caring for Mr Dick, a pleasant simpleton. She is as eccentric as ever, but takes him in, as he had hoped, and dismisses the Murdstones from their responsibility for him. She also arranges for him to live in Canterbury with her lawyer, Mr Wickfield, and his lovely daughter, Agnes, and to attend old Doctor Strong's excellent school there. In Canterbury, David also meets Wickfield's sinister clerk, the 'umble' Uriah Heep, and renews his friendship with the Micawbers when they happen to pass through town.

David grows up, successfully completes his education, and is to spend some time 'looking about' for a career. Passing through London, he happens to meet Steerforth, who takes him to visit his mother and her ardent companion, Rosa Dartle. David was on his way to revisit Mr Peggotty and his household at Yarmouth, and now takes Steerforth with him. They find little Em'ly grown up and engaged to Ham. Peggotty has married Barkis the carrier: their courtship was aided by David occasionally acting as Barkis's messenger to Peggotty.

David is articled to Spenlow and Jorkins as an apprentice proctor in Doctors' Commons. He takes rooms in London, where he entertains Steerforth, drunkenly; and later invites the Micawbers, still short of money, and their new lodger, Traddles. David meets Dora Spenlow and instantly falls desperately in love with her. After her birthday picnic, they are secretly engaged.

David returns briefly to Yarmouth, as Barkis is dying. While he is there, Mr Peggotty's household is most unhappily upset by Emily's running away with Steerforth. Mr Peggotty resolves to follow her, find her, and bring her back. He meets, unsatisfactorily, proud Mrs Steerforth and the infuriated Rosa Dartle.

Aunt Betsey arrives in London with Mr Dick, and announces that she is ruined. David starts work with great determination, as a part-time secretary to Doctor Strong. At the same time he teaches himself shorthand. After many struggles, he becomes a parliamentary reporter. Mr Spenlow has learned of his daughter's secret engagement, through her companion, Jane Murdstone, and tells David he forbids it. But he dies suddenly that night, and Dora moves to live with her aunts. David is allowed to visit her there. Eventually his hopes are fulfilled and he and Dora are married.

Previously, Uriah Heep appeared in London, seeming to have Mr Wickfield in his power, and still hoping, as he has told David, to marry Agnes. After David's marriage, he returns, and makes unpleasant suggestions concerning Doctor Strong's young wife Annie and her idle cousin Jack Maldon. Doctor Strong denies these, but a shadow falls between him and Annie. With the sensitive help of Mr Dick, the truth is revealed, and they are reconciled.

From Steerforth's servant, Littimer, David hears that Steerforth has abandoned Emily. He passes this news on to Mr Peggotty, who occasionally returns to London during his quest for his niece. Together, they find her unfortunate friend, Martha Endell, and ask her to help them. When Emily returns to London, Martha finds her, and at last she and Mr Peggotty are happily re-united. They decide to emigrate to Australia, taking with them Mrs Gummidge and, eventually, Martha as well.

For some time, Micawber, now working as a clerk for Heep, behaves strangely. Then he calls David and his aunt to Canterbury, and, with his usual great eloquence, accuses Heep of many frauds and crimes against Mr Wickfield. With the help of the reliable Traddles, Uriah

Heep is crushed. Micawber is lent money to ease his financial difficulties; he and his family accept the suggestion of emigrating.

David has become a successful author, and gives up his job as a parliamentary reporter. His marriage to Dora, though happy, is marred because she is so completely impractical. Realising that it is selfish to try to 'form her mind', David is reconciled and loves her for herself, but still feels a sense of loss and incompleteness in their relationship. Dora loses a child and is afterwards very ill. Her illness continues: she weakens slowly, and dies.

David decides to take his grief abroad. But first, he takes a message from Emily to Ham in Yarmouth. He arrives there during a great storm, and witnesses the drowning of Steerforth in a wreck just off the coast, and the death of Ham in attempting to rescue him. He breaks the news to Mrs Steerforth and Rosa Dartle, but conceals it from Mr Peggotty and Emily. He says farewell to them, and to the Micawbers, before they all depart for Australia.

David wanders sadly abroad. His reputation as a novelist grows. He is consoled by a letter from Agnes, and returns to Britain where he finds Traddles now practising as a lawyer and happily married at last to his Sophy. With Traddles, he visits a prison and finds that two of the convicts are Heep and Littimer.

David realises what he had long been blind to: that he has always loved Agnes Wickfield, and that she has always been the light of his life. His 'undisciplined heart' had led him astray. Now he is sure that Agnes is involved with someone else, and decides he must not interfere. At last this misunderstanding is cleared up. David and Agnes declare their mutual love, and are married. Agnes reveals that this was Dora's dying wish.

Ten years later, Mr Peggotty returns from Australia, with news of the emigrants, who have all made a success of their new lives. Micawber has even become a magistrate. David remains very happily married to Agnes. Aunt Betsey and Peggotty help to look after their children. With Agnes, David Copperfield has established himself and achieved his happiness.

The summary above gives only the barest outline of what happens in *David Copperfield*. The following chapter summaries give a more detailed version of the story, and some of the mood of the novel. But it is most important to remember that neither summary can replace the novel itself. These summaries are only an aid to revision, not at all a substitute for reading *David Copperfield*.

Detailed summaries

Chapter 1: I am born

Young, inexperienced Clara Copperfield, expecting a child, is sitting in her home, Blunderstone Rookery, one Friday evening. She is sad and confused, mourning her husband, who died six months before. She is surprised by the arrival of his eccentric aunt, Betsey Trotwood, who firmly believes the expected child will be a girl, whom she says she intends to look after personally. But the child born later that evening is a boy, later named David Copperfield. When she hears this news from the doctor (Mr Chillip), Aunt Betsey departs disgusted.

NOTES AND GLOSSARY

a caul: a thin inner tissue covering the unborn child, sometimes emerging on the baby's head at birth. Often believed to be a lucky charm, especially against drowning

a Baboo ... a Begum: an Indian gentleman and lady

a Saracen's head in a Dutch clock: cheap clocks, often decorated with drawings

weeds: widow's mourning clothes

the ghost in Hamlet: a reference to Shakespeare's *Hamlet*; the ghost appears in Acts I and III

Chapter 2: I observe

David recalls his 'very earliest impressions' of his simple, happy, early childhood: his home; going to church; his mother and Peggotty. Mr Murdstone appears darkly in this contented world and begins to court Mrs Copperfield, making Peggotty and David uneasy. Murdstone takes David on a ride to Lowestoft. David tells his mother what Murdstone and his friends there said about her. Peggotty arranges to take David to her brother's home in Yarmouth (a port on the east coast of England) for a fortnight.

NOTES AND GLOSSARY

Lazarus: the story of Lazarus being raised from the dead is in the Bible, John chapter 11

shaver: a young chap

Brooks of Sheffield: a name intended to hide from David a reference to himself. It appropriately suggests sharpness: Sheffield, in Yorkshire, was (and still is) a centre for the manufacture of knives and cutlery

Chapter 3: I have a change

Peggotty and David arrive at her brother's home in Yarmouth, an old grounded boat. David meets Mr Peggotty, his nephew Ham and pretty niece little Em'ly, and the forlorn widow Mrs Gummidge. They all live in the fascinating old boat, under Mr Peggotty's kindly protection. David has a fine time and falls childishly in love with little Em'ly. He returns to Blunderstone with Peggotty to find a grave change: during his absence, his mother has married Mr Murdstone.

NOTES AND GLOSSARY

Yarmouth bloater: a famous Yarmouth fish product; by extension, a native of Yarmouth

Aladdin's palace, roc's egg and all: Aladdin was a character in the fantastic stories of the *Arabian Nights*. The roc was a fabulous bird, also mentioned in the *Arabian Nights*

all-fours: a card game

the house: the parish workhouse for the poor

Chapter 4: I fall into disgrace

David goes tearfully to his room where Murdstone confronts him and his mother. Murdstone's sister Jane arrives and soon takes over housekeeping from David's mother, whose protests are coldly overcome by Murdstone. David is increasingly kept from his mother's love, and grows miserable. Only his enjoyment of a collection of novels cheers him up. But he fails again at his lessons, Murdstone beats him and David bites his hand. He is kept in his room, disgraced, for five days, and then sent away from home to a school near London.

NOTES AND GLOSSARY

a perfect Lark: a very early riser, since the lark is known for its early rising

in the midst of the Disciples: reference to another Bible story, Matthew 18

Roderick Random, Peregrine Pickle, Humphrey Clinker: novels published respectively in 1748, 1751 and 1771 by Tobias Smollett (1721-71), a Scottish author

Tom Jones: a novel (1749) by Henry Fielding (1707-54)

The Vicar of Wakefield: a novel (1766) by Oliver Goldsmith (1728-74), an Irish author

Robinson Crusoe: a novel (1720) by Daniel Defoe (1660-1731)

Don Quixote: Cervantes's famous Spanish novel (1605)

Gil Blas: tale by the French author Le Sage, set in Spain (1715-35)

Tom Pipes, Strap, Commodore Trunnion, Mr Pickle: all characters in Smollett's novels

Chapter 5: I am sent away from home

Peggotty stops David and says goodbye to him. She makes an impression on Barkis, the carrier. He encourages David to pass on to her the message 'Barkis is willin''. In Yarmouth David is cheated by a waiter. Arrived in London, the schoolmaster, Mell, takes him to Salem House school. On the way they stop at an alms-house where Mell's mother lives. The school is on holiday, and David wonders what the boys will say about him when they return and read the sign he has been made to wear: 'Take care of him. He bites'.

NOTES AND GLOSSARY
a set of castors: usually containers for salt, pepper, and mustard
cowpock: a disease, a mild form of smallpox
wittles: food
send me to Coventry: to send someone to Coventry is to ignore them completely and exclude them from society

Chapter 6: I enlarge my circle of acquaintance

David has a frightening interview with Creakle, the harsh headmaster, and meets his family. He meets the boys as they return, notably Tommy Traddles and Steerforth, who says he will 'take care of' David and of his money, but spends it all on food for the boys in his dormitory. David learns from them about the school and the cruelty of the headmaster.

NOTES AND GLOSSARY
a Tartar: a fierce, nasty person
prog: food
parlour-boarder: a pupil who ate his meals with the headmaster

Chapter 7: My 'first half' at Salem House

The school term begins, and with it the suffering of the pupils, especially Traddles. Every night in their dormitory, Steerforth listens to David telling the stories of the novels he has read. David has also told Steerforth that Mell's mother lives in an alms-house. One afternoon Steerforth confronts and insults Mell with this fact. Creakle, over-hearing this, dismisses Mell immediately. Mr Peggotty and Ham come to visit David, and he introduces them to Steerforth. At last the term ends, and David travels home.

NOTES AND GLOSSARY

exordium:	(*Latin*) an introductory speech
parts:	abilities
Beadle:	a church officer
Arabian Nights ... Sultana Scheherazade:	the Sultana Scheherazade was the story-teller in the *Arabian Nights*. She survived by relating uncompleted stories every night, leaving the King in suspense until the next instalment
Alguazil:	a Spanish law-officer. *Gil Blas* was set in Spain
a Brick:	a good fellow

Chapter 8: My holidays. Especially one happy afternoon

On his way home, David is asked by Barkis to take another message to Peggotty. He arrives home at Blunderstone to find that the Murdstones are out. So he passes a very happy afternoon with Peggotty and his mother, who has had a baby during his absence. They discuss the Murdstones, and Barkis. The Murdstones return, and their chill presence spoils the rest of David's holiday. He is allowed no freedom or enjoyment and is almost glad to return to school. He looks back on his mother, holding up his baby brother in farewell.

NOTES AND GLOSSARY

some cats:	unpleasant people, in this case the Murdstones
a daymare:	an unhappy daydream
threading my grandmother's needle:	a way of saying that David's thoughts are wandering

---

Chapter 9: I have a memorable birthday

Two months after he returns to school, on his birthday, David learns from Mrs Creakle that his mother has died. He is desolate, and weeps. On his way home for the funeral, he is met in Yarmouth by the undertaker, Mr Omer. David goes to Omer's shop where he is a little disturbed by the cheerfulness of the funeral preparations. Omer adds to his grief by telling him that his baby brother has also died. With Omer, his daughter Minnie and her lover Joram, David goes on to Blunderstone, where he is sadly met by Peggotty. They attend the funeral. David is consoled by Mr Chillip, and by Peggotty, who tells him how his mother, 'uncertain in her mind, and not happy', slowly faded and finally died in Peggotty's arms.

NOTES AND GLOSSARY

a porpoise: here used to mean that Mr Omer is very fat

to bait the horse: to rest and feed the horse

Chapter 10: I become neglected, and am provided for

Mr Murdstone dismisses Peggotty, but she is allowed to take David with her to Yarmouth for another fortnight's holiday at her brother's house. On the way there, Barkis happily meets Peggotty again. Later, he starts courting her, and they are married. After the simple ceremony, they take David and little Em'ly on a day's outing. At Yarmouth, David also meets Mr Peggotty, Ham, and Mrs Gummidge again. When he returns to Blunderstone, he is neglected and ignored by the Murdstones, and leads a sad, lonely life. Mr Murdstone owns a wine business, Murdstone and Grinby's, and David is told that he is to go and work there. So he has to leave Blunderstone for London.

NOTES AND GLOSSARY

'a young Roeshus': Roscius was a famous Roman actor, and Barkis's comparison is a sort of compliment

a very Gunpowder Plot: the Gunpowder Plot was an attempt to blow up Parliament on 5 November 1605. Reference to it here emphasises the complication and difficulty of Peggotty's plans

Chapter 11: I begin life on my own account, and don't like it

David starts work at Murdstone and Grinby's, washing and labelling bottles. He is very miserable in this unpleasant situation. His hopes of progress in life seem lost. He meets the extraordinary Mr Micawber and arranges to lodge in his house. He meets the Micawber family and soon learns that they are seriously short of money. David recalls his wanderings, poor and lonely, around London. Mr Micawber is eventually arrested for his debts. He is later joined in prison by the rest of his family, and he draws up a petition against imprisonment for debt. David moves into a small room of his own. He continues his solitary London life, and his wretched work at the warehouse.

NOTES AND GLOSSARY

hind: a servant or labourer

surtout: an overcoat

tights: tight trousers

a quizzing-glass: an eye-glass

experientia does it: Mrs Micawber misquotes *experientia docet*, Latin for 'experience teaches'

the modern Babylon: Mr Micawber's name for London
saveloy: a kind of spicy sausage
alamode beef-house: alamode (*French: à la mode*) beef was a kind of meat stew
egg-hot: a hot drink made from beer, eggs, sugar, and nutmeg

Chapter 12: Liking life on my own account no better, I form a great resolution

Micawber is released from prison. David celebrates with Mrs Micawber, who loudly affirms that she 'never will desert Mr Micawber', and explains that the family have decided to go to Plymouth, expecting that 'something will turn up' there. David parts from them sadly, and is left alone. He remembers his mother's stories about his Aunt Betsey, learns from Peggotty that she lives near Dover, and decides to run away from Murdstone and Grinby's and look for her there. Some money he borrowed from Peggotty is stolen, along with his box. He has to set out for Dover on foot, penniless and with only the clothes he is wearing.

NOTES AND GLOSSARY
flip: a drink made from eggs and hot beer, wine or spirits
punch: a drink made from wine or spirits, flavoured with fruit juices and spices
a tanner: sixpence
pollis: police

Chapter 13: The sequel of my resolution

During his long walk from London to Dover (70 miles), David has to spend the nights in the open (once near his old school), and sell his clothes to get enough money to eat. On one occasion, a most peculiar shopkeeper frightens and tries to cheat him. When he arrives in Dover, he asks about his aunt and eventually finds her cottage. Filthy and exhausted, he explains to her who he is, and tells his story. Miss Betsey Trotwood is still eccentric, and often dashes out to chase passing donkeys from her lawn. And she relies on the advice of simple-minded Mr Dick, who also lives in the cottage, and suggests what she should do with David: wash him and put him to bed.

NOTES AND GLOSSARY
slop-shops: shops selling cheap or second-hand clothing
What lay are you upon?: What's your job?
prig: a tinker, or a thief

fly-drivers:	a fly was a kind of carriage
Cain:	In the Bible (see Genesis 4) Cain was an outcast and wanderer after he murdered his brother Abel

---

Chapter 14: My Aunt makes up her mind about me

Aunt Betsey tells David she has written to Mr Murdstone about him. David gets to know Mr Dick and learns how King Charles's head keeps appearing in the memorial he is writing. But David is sternly assured by his aunt that Mr Dick is not at all insane. She explains how she came to take care of him. The Murdstones arrive and give their very low opinion of David. But Miss Betsey, with astonishing vigour, states her low opinion of the Murdstones, and they leave, giving up their responsibility for David. His aunt accepts him, calls him Trotwood (or Trot) Copperfield, and a happier part of his life begins.

NOTES AND GLOSSARY

Phoebus:	(*Latin*) the sun
Bedlam:	Bethlehem Hospital, a famous lunatic asylum
a natural:	a fool or madman
Franklin:	Benjamin Franklin (1706-90), the American politician, inventor, and scientist

---

Chapter 15: I make another beginning

David is pleased that his aunt is growing fond of him, and delighted when she suggests that he should go to school. He has befriended Mr Dick, who is sorry to see him leave for Canterbury, where his schooling is arranged by Aunt Betsey's lawyer, Mr Wickfield. It is also agreed that David will be a lodger in Wickfield's house. There he meets Wickfield's 'placid and sweet' daughter Agnes, but is made uneasy by his sinister assistant, Uriah Heep.

Chapter 16: I am a new boy in more senses than one

Wickfield takes David to Doctor Strong's fine school. Here he meets the gentle old Doctor, and his pretty young wife, Annie. He overhears Wickfield and Doctor Strong planning a future for her cousin, Jack Maldon, who appears at Wickfield's that evening. Starting school is strange for David, as he is still haunted by memories of his recent unhappy experiences, but he is soon at his ease there and works hard. Like all the schoolboys, he admires Doctor Strong. David talks to Uriah Heep, who explains how 'umble' he is. At a party in honour of Jack Maldon's departure for India, Annie's possessive mother, Mrs Markleham ('the old soldier'), tells the story of her daughter's marriage to Doctor Strong. Jack Maldon leaves, but David notices that something strange has happened. And Annie is found to have fainted. Later, David finds her and the Doctor closely together in a memorable scene.

NOTES AND GLOSSARY

Doctor Watts:	Isaac Watts (1674–1748), a famous writer of hymns
Tidd's Practice:	a handbook for lawyers
articles:	a lawyer's apprenticeship
post-chaise:	a kind of carriage
Sindbad:	Sindbad was a wandering sailor whose adventurous travels are told in the *Arabian Nights*
Rajah:	an Indian nobleman

Chapter 17: Somebody turns up

David writes to Peggotty, and receives news of Yarmouth from her. Mr Dick begins regular visits to Canterbury, and grows popular around the school. From him David hears of a strange man who has appeared near Aunt Betsey's cottage and frightened her. David goes for tea with Uriah and his mother, Mrs Heep. They encourage him to talk too much about himself, his relations, and the Wickfields. Mr Micawber appears by chance at the door and is introduced to the Heeps. David visits Mrs Micawber, who explains how they happen to be in Canterbury. Mr Micawber and Uriah later seem to become friends. David has an enjoyable farewell dinner with the Micawbers, but receives a despairing letter from them next morning. However, he sees them leaving Canterbury for London, apparently very cheerfully.

NOTES AND GLOSSARY

escritoire:	(*French*) a writing-desk
promissory notes, notes of hand:	promises to repay debts
dumb-waiter:	a stand for several dishes of food
eulogium:	(*Latin*) a speech of praise

Chapter 18: A retrospect

With warmth and amusement, David recalls his growth 'from childhood up to youth': his progress at school; his young love for Miss Shepherd; his defeat in a fight with a young butcher. He becomes head boy at school; falls deeply in boyish love with a Miss Larkins; dreams of her and dances with her. His foolish ideal is shattered when she marries someone else; however he recovers, fights the butcher again, and wins.

NOTES AND GLOSSARY
a spencer:	a short overcoat
the stocks:	a method for straightening the feet used in nineteenth century schools
the apparition of an armed head in Macbeth:	a reference to Shakespeare's *Macbeth*, Act IV, Scene 1
bear's grease:	used as hair-oil
spoony:	foolish, silly

Chapter 19: I look about me, and make a discovery

David leaves school. He considers his future, with his aunt, who tells him her hopes for his character, and suggests that while they think, he should return briefly to Yarmouth for a holiday. On his way there, he visits Agnes in Canterbury, tells her how much he trusts her, and discusses with her Mr Wickfield's drinking and loss of responsibility. He also visits Doctor Strong, and hears that Jack Maldon is returning from India. Wickfield seems to suspect Annie Strong. David goes on to London, and his treatment on the way there, and at an inn, reminds him of his youth and inexperience. Returning ·from the theatre, he happens to meet Steerforth, now a student at Oxford.

NOTES AND GLOSSARY
a Brazier:	a brassworker
a pretty kettle of fish:	a fuss
a Suffolk Punch:	a breed of horse
Box Seat:	the box seat was next to the coachman, and was a favourite position
taters:	potatoes
patten:	an overshoe, with a thick wooden or metal sole

Chapter 20: Steerforth's home

David agrees to look around London with Steerforth, and to spend a few days at his home in Highgate. There he meets Steerforth's devoted mother, and her companion, Rosa Dartle. David is delighted to hear that Steerforth might go to Yarmouth with him, to visit the Peggottys. He shares Mrs Steerforth's praise of her son, observes Rosa Dartle's dark energy, and learns what caused her scar.

NOTES AND GLOSSARY
King Charles on horseback:	a statue
see the lions:	see the sights of London. Lions were kept in the Tower of London at this time

a panorama: a wall painting giving a large view. It also came to mean a mechanically produced picture show
the old writing on the wall: an omen, a sign foretelling disaster. See the Bible, Daniel 5

Chapter 21: Little Em'ly

David spends a pleasant week at Highgate. He meets Littimer, Steerforth's respectable servant. Steerforth comes to Yarmouth, where David first re-visits Omer, the undertaker, and hears from him the general opinion of little Em'ly, now grown up and apprenticed to him as a dressmaker. Then David visits Peggotty, now of course Mrs Barkis. They are delighted to meet again. David talks to her husband, who is now kept in bed with rheumatism, and is very careful of his money. Steerforth arrives and he and David have dinner with Peggotty. Later, they go to Mr Peggotty's house and find everyone, even Mrs Gummidge, happily celebrating Emily's engagement to Ham. They join in the celebrations, and Steerforth uses his charm.

NOTES AND GLOSSARY
livery: servants' clothing
magpie proceedings: hoarding, like a magpie
tarpaulin: Mr Peggotty means 'a sailor'
the murder's out: all is revealed
Hollands: Hollands gin, a grain spirit
chuckle-headed: simple-minded

Chapter 22: Some old scenes, and some new people

Steerforth meets and works with the fishermen, while David stays with Peggotty and re-visits Blunderstone. Returning from one of these visits, he finds Steerforth at Mr Peggotty's house, in a very dark and self-doubting mood. Cheering up, he tells David he has bought a boat, which is to be re-named the 'Little Em'ly'. He mentions that Littimer has come to Yarmouth. They meet Ham and Emily, who are being followed by a strange young woman. After dinner, David meets Miss Mowcher, an extraordinary and talkative dwarf who grooms Steerforth. Later, David returns to Barkis's house. He finds Ham outside, and learns from him that Emily is talking to Martha Endell, an unfortunate girl whom she used to know and now helps with money to go to London. Emily tells Ham that she is not worthy of his love.

NOTES AND GLOSSARY
hipped: gloomy
like Macbeth: both Steerforth's quotations here are from Shakespeare, *Macbeth*, Act III Scene 4

the Ixions:	Ixion was a Greek mythic character who was punished by being eternally bound to a revolving wheel
downy:	alert and knowing
Walker:	'Hookey Walker' was a nineteenth century expression for lies and nonsense
gammon and spinnage:	nonsense and pretence
the polar regions:	the top of Steerforth's head
Madagascar liquid:	hair oil
a Griffin:	a fabulous monster
Did he sip every flower ... requited:	Miss Mowcher is quoting from *The Beggar's Opera* (1728), by John Gay
volatile:	lively
Fatima:	a character from the fairy story, *Bluebeard*, who suffered for her curiosity
noddle:	the head
mizzle:	to depart
five bob:	five shillings
Bob swore:	French for 'good evening' is *bon soir*
a scientific cupper:	one who used a nineteenth century medical technique for drawing blood

Chapter 23: I corroborate Mr Dick, and choose a profession

Steerforth and David regretfully leave Yarmouth. Littimer remains. David consults Steerforth about his aunt's suggestion that he should become a proctor in Doctors' Commons. In London he meets his Aunt Betsey again. On their way to arrange for David's apprenticeship at Doctors' Commons, his aunt encounters a strange man. They depart in a coach, and David, left alone, recalls Mr Dick's story of the strange man at Dover. At Doctors' Commons, Mr Spenlow arranges for David's training with his firm, Spenlow and Jorkins. Aunt Betsey also arranges rooms for David, and he meets the caretaker, Mrs Crupp. Aunt Betsey returns to Dover.

NOTES AND GLOSSARY

Doctors' Commons:	as Steerforth partly explains, this was a collective name for several rather old-fashioned law courts, mostly dealing with shipping business, church matters, and wills
the giants of St. Dunstan's:	mechanical figures who struck the hours on a bell at St. Dunstan's Church in Fleet Street
an Arches day:	a day when cases were heard in the Court of Arches (the Church Court)
Punch:	a comic puppet figure

Chapter 24: My first dissipation

David is a little lonely in his new London home, but when Steerforth arrives unexpectedly, he arranges a dinner for him and his two friends that evening. David drinks too much wine. Later, they all go to the theatre, and David is unlucky enough to meet Agnes there while he is very drunk. The next morning he suffers great remorse and a terrible hangover.

NOTES AND GLOSSARY
Lares: Lares and Penates were the household gods of ancient Rome

Chapter 25: Good and bad angels

David receives a note from Agnes. She is staying at Mr Waterbrook's, and he visits her there that afternoon. She warns him against Steerforth, and tells him how Uriah Heep has gained power over her father, and is about to become his partner. He is invited to the Waterbrook's house for dinner next day. Among a mixed company, he meets again his old schoolfriend, Traddles. David also meet Uriah Heep, and invites him back to his rooms for coffee. From him, David hears more about Wickfield's carelessness, and is outraged to learn that Uriah wants to marry Agnes.

NOTES AND GLOSSARY
Titans: in Greek mythology a legendary race of giants
ticket-porter: a messenger
blood: aristocratic descent
ogres: fairy tale monsters who ate men
beau-ideal: (*French*) highest ideal
a pony-shay: a kind of carriage

Chapter 26: I fall into captivity

David uneasily watches Uriah Heep and Agnes leave London. To celebrate his being articled to the firm, Mr Spenlow invites David to his house at Norwood for the weekend. On the way, Spenlow explains and praises Doctors' Commons. At Norwood, David meets his daughter Dora, and instantly falls in love with her, although he is distressed to find that her companion turns out to be Miss Murdstone. She suggests that they conceal their past differences, and David agrees. He talks briefly to Dora. Returned to London, he is in a state of such forlorn love-sickness that even Mrs Crupp comments upon it.

NOTES AND GLOSSARY

Rufus:	(*from the Latin*) a red-haired person
phaeton:	a kind of carriage
the Consistory:	one of the courts in Doctors' Commons
a Sylph:	an airy spirit
a life-preserver:	a stick or club
Trinity Masters:	the 'Elder brethren', experts on shipping, who govern Trinity House, an organisation responsible for the official regulation of shipping around the British coasts
cardamums:	spices

Chapter 27: Tommy Traddles

David goes to visit his old friend Traddles, and is astonished to discover him lodging with the Micawbers, whom he also meets again. They still have money problems. Traddles explains that he is engaged, and has also had to save and do extra work to meet the expenses of his training as a lawyer.

NOTES AND GLOSSARY

reading for the bar . . . keep my terms:	training as a lawyer
in statu quo:	(*Latin*) Mr Micawber's way of saying he is quite well
hard-bake:	a sweet
Bow-Street officer:	an eighteenth or nineteenth century policeman; so called from the magistrate's court in Bow Street, London.

Chapter 28: Mr Micawber's gauntlet

The Micawbers and Traddles come to dinner in David's rooms. The food is badly prepared, so the guests take over the cooking themselves. As they are doing so, Littimer mysteriously appears, looking for Steerforth. Mrs Micawber explains her opinion that her husband should encourage something to 'turn up' by advertising his talents in the newspapers. Very shortly after their departure, Steerforth arrives from Yarmouth, with a letter from Peggotty. David learns that Barkis is very ill, and decides to go to Yarmouth. Mr Micawber has left David another despairing letter, saying that he is again bankrupt, and cannot repay his debts to Traddles.

NOTES AND GLOSSARY

the Hymeneal altar:	the wedding altar, from Hymen, the Greek god of marriage

a Devil:	a grill, cooked over the fire
We twae hae run . . . gowans fine:	a quotation from *Auld Lang Syne*, a famous song by Robert Burns (1759–96), which David sang once before with the Micawbers (Chapter 17)
a Sybarite:	a lover of pleasure and luxury; from Sybaris, a town in Italy famed for the luxurious habits of its citizens
a Bacchanal:	a drunken reveller. Bacchus was the Greek God of wine

Chapter 29: I visit Steerforth at his home, again

Steerforth has persuaded David to come to his Highgate home again, so he gets leave from Doctors' Commons. At Highgate he meets Mrs Steerforth again, and Rosa Dartle, who seems very suspicious. She questions David strangely about what Steerforth is doing, and darkly hints at division between Mrs Steerforth and her son. Steerforth charms and calms Rosa, who sings. But when he touches her, she strikes him. Before David leaves for Yarmouth, there are suggestions of an approaching change for Steerforth.

Chapter 30: A loss

At Yarmouth, David hears from Omer of Emily's unsettled state of mind. He learns of Barkis's serious condition, and hurries to his house, where he finds Mr Peggotty, Ham, and Emily. She behaves oddly, seeming fearful and very uneasy. Peggotty takes David up to see Barkis, her husband. Barkis recognises David briefly, before dying as the tide is turning.

NOTES AND GLOSSARY

to move to:	to nod or bow to
srub:	'shrub'—fruit juice, sugar, and rum

Chapter 31: A greater loss

Barkis is buried in Blunderstone. He left a lot of money, and David uses his new knowledge to explain his will. David is with Mrs Gummidge, Peggotty, and Mr Peggotty, at the latter's house, when Ham arrives in great distress with a farewell note from Emily and the news that she has run away. It seems Steerforth has taken her. Mr Peggotty, grief-stricken, resolves to go and search for her and bring her back. Mrs Gummidge sympathetically stops him from leaving immediately.

NOTES AND GLOSSARY

visionary Strap . . . yore: a reference to David's vivid imagination of the books he read as a child, mentioned in Chapter 4

chay: a kind of carriage

Chapter 32: The beginning of a long journey

David finds Ham and Mr Peggotty walking on the beach, and hears their plans for the future. Mrs Gummidge is to remain looking after his house while Mr Peggotty seeks Emily 'through the wureld'. Ham is to stay with his aunt, Peggotty. Mrs Gummidge casts off her sorrows and makes herself very useful. Miss Mowcher appears at Peggotty's late one night, and chides David for his poor opinion of her. She goes on to explain how Steerforth acted in running off with Emily, and the part Littimer played in his plans. Next day, David and Peggotty, and Mr Peggotty, go to London. With Mr Peggotty, David visits Mrs Steerforth. They are received with cold pride. Rosa Dartle vents on David her fury of frustration about Steerforth and Emily. Mr Peggotty sets off on his search for his niece.

Chapter 33: Blissful

David is still enormously in love with Dora Spenlow. He confesses this to Peggotty, who is in London while he settles the details of Barkis's will. During this business, they meet Mr Murdstone (who has come to Doctors' Commons for a marriage licence) and have an angry conversation with him. David discusses the failings of Doctors' Commons with Mr Spenlow, who invites him to Dora's birthday picnic. After an awkward start, this turns out to be a very happy occasion. David meets Dora's friend Julia Mills, who invites him to visit her London home while Dora is staying there. He does so, and, ignoring the uproar of her dog Jip, declares his great love to Dora. They are engaged. This is to be kept secret from Mr Spenlow. David warmly remembers the simple happiness of this time.

NOTES AND GLOSSARY

The Bench . . . The Bar: judges and their courts

proved the will: had it accepted as valid and correct

the Surrogate: the official who issued marriage licences

the Prerogative Office: where wills were 'proved'

a pluralist: a holder of more than one office at a time

a Voice from the Cloister: a voice of someone who has retired from the world (usually by entering a religious order)

cocked-hat note: a note folded into a triangular shape, like a cocked hat

Chapter 34: My Aunt astonishes me

David writes to Agnes, explaining his love for Dora. Mrs Crupp resents Peggotty and stops work. Traddles visits David, and tells him about his fiancée Sophy, and about the renewed financial difficulties of the Micawbers. Peggotty helps Traddles by buying back possessions he lost because of his involvement in Micawber's debts. On their return, Peggotty and David are astonished to find Aunt Betsey, Mr Dick, and their luggage occupying David's rooms. Betsey Trotwood explains that she is ruined.

Chapter 35: Depression

David upsets Mr Dick by telling him what 'ruined' means. Aunt Betsey begins to approve of Peggotty. David tells her about Dora. He considers what poverty will mean to him, and tries unsuccessfully to cancel his articles to recover some of the premium. He meets Agnes and returns to his rooms with her. Aunt Betsey gives Agnes an explanation of how she lost all her money. Agnes suggests that David could work as a secretary for Doctor Strong, who has retired and come to live near London. Mr Wickfield arrives at David's rooms looking unwell. Uriah Heep, now his partner, is with him, and disgusts everybody. David dines with Wickfield and Agnes, who is more radiant than ever.

NOTES AND GLOSSARY

a 'British Judy':	a British jury
Tom Tiddler:	a children's game about sunken treasure
galvanic:	galvanism was a kind of electric shock; 'galvanic' suggests convulsive movement

Chapter 36: Enthusiasm

David is very determined to prove himself, and visits Doctor Strong, who gladly agrees to employ him as a secretary in his work on the dictionary. He meets Mrs Strong again. She seems uneasy in the presence of Jack Maldon, recently returned from India. David now makes himself work very hard. He goes to visit Traddles, and they content Mr Dick by arranging a job for him, copying writing. David decides to learn shorthand and become a parliamentary reporter. With Traddles, he attends another of the Micawbers' farewell parties. They are going to Canterbury, as Mr Micawber has been employed by Uriah Heep as a confidential clerk. Micawber seems to pay his debts to Traddles, but only by means of further promises.

NOTES AND GLOSSARY
a little Patent place: an easy job in the Patent Office
the Phoenix: a mythic bird, supposed to burn itself to death in a fire from whose ashes a new Phoenix arises
the woolsack: seat of the Lord Chancellor in the House of Lords

Chapter 37: A little cold water

Aunt Betsey settles Mrs Crupp and improves David's rooms. Peggotty returns to Yarmouth, first offering to help David with money. He visits Dora at Miss Mills's and alarms her by explaining his financial problems. He finds her 'a little impracticable', and unable to listen to his suggestions about economy and carefulness. Julia Mills agrees to try to bring housekeeping to Dora's notice. David continues working very hard, and sometimes thinks over a little fearfully the mutual love between himself and Dora.

NOTES AND GLOSSARY
graminivorous: grass-eating
a navigator: a 'navvy', a manual labourer

Chapter 38: A dissolution of partnership

David puts into practice his determination to learn shorthand. He struggles, and Traddles helps him. Miss Murdstone has discovered David's letters to Dora and informed Mr Spenlow, who confronts David with them. Mr Spenlow considers his affair with Dora 'youthful nonsense' and tells David he must forget it. That evening, however, Mr Spenlow dies suddenly. It is discovered that he has left no will, and was not very rich when he died. Dora goes to live with two old maiden aunts in Putney. David hears news of her through Julia Mills.

NOTES AND GLOSSARY
an Egyptian Temple in itself: very difficult and complicated, like the hieroglyphs in an Egyptian temple
Enfield's Speaker: a popular handbook of public speaking
Mr Pitt ... Mr Canning: all famous British politicians in the late eighteenth and early nineteenth centuries
nailed all sorts of colours ... mast: changed sides and opinions very frequently
the Dragon of Wantley: a humorous song about a monster in Yorkshire that ate cattle and children

Chapter 39: Wickfield and Heep

David briefly criticises Doctors' Commons. Aunt Betsey decides she ought to send him to Dover on business about her cottage. Returning through Canterbury, he talks to Mr Micawber, now working at Wickfield and Heep's. He seems uneasy and reserved about his new job, but tells David how Uriah has helped him with money. David sees Agnes and tells her again how much he relies upon her. She advises him to write to Dora's aunts. Uriah suspects David of being his rival for Agnes, and sets his mother to watch them, until David reveals his engagement to Dora. Uriah explains the nature and origin of his 'umbleness' at school. His power over Wickfield is greater than ever, but Uriah goes too far by revealing his intentions towards his daughter Agnes. Wickfield is very angry, and criticises himself for his weakness and errors. Uriah is 'umble' again, but still confident. David is afraid for Agnes, but she reassures him. He says goodbye to her and leaves Canterbury in the morning.

NOTES AND GLOSSARY
stock: a neckcloth
foundation school: a school for the poor
no squares broke between us: no permanent harm done to our association

Chapter 40: The wanderer

David sends his letter to Dora's aunts. Aunt Betsey is upset by David's account of his visit to Canterbury. On his way home from Doctor Strong's one snowy night, he chances to meet Martha Endell, and, immediately afterwards, Mr Peggotty, who has returned briefly from his search for Emily. They go to an inn, and Mr Peggotty tells David about his wanderings in France, Italy, and Switzerland, everywhere asking for Emily. She has written him letters in which money was enclosed, and Mr Peggotty is absolutely determined to return it. Their conversation is overheard by Martha Endell, whom David sees listening outside the inn door. Mr Peggotty is leaving again in the morning to renew his search, and he and David part on Westminster Bridge.

Chapter 41: Dora's Aunts

The Misses Spenlow, Dora's aunts, invite David to come and visit them, with a friend. He misses the advice of Julia Mills, who is going to India with her father. He visits the aunts with Traddles, who explains his own difficulties in persuading his fiancée Sophy's family to part with her. With the Misses Spenlow, he has a prolonged and delicate interview.

It is finally arranged that he will be allowed to visit them, and see Dora, twice a week. Miss Trotwood and the Misses Spenlow also begin to exchange visits. David is happily reunited with Dora. He loves her as much as ever, but is sometimes uneasy at her acting, as her aunts seem to expect, a little as a child.

NOTES AND GLOSSARY

fretful porcupine:	Traddles refers to Shakespeare, *Hamlet*, Act I, Scene 5; 'And each particular hair to stand on end/Like quills upon the fretful porcupine'
short whist:	a card game
Bath water:	the mineral water from the health resort at Bath

Chapter 42: Mischief

David recalls his determination, and his hard work, and the principles on which these were based. Agnes and Mr Wickfield come to visit Doctor Strong. Mrs Heep and Uriah also come to London. Heep makes unpleasant remarks to David about Jack Maldon and Annie Strong. David takes Agnes to meet Dora and is delighted by their appreciation of one another. On returning to Doctor Strong's house he discovers Uriah has told the Doctor of his suspicions of an affair between Mrs Strong and Jack Maldon, and urges Wickfield and even David to confirm them. The Doctor, greatly moved, honourably refuses to doubt his wife, and blames himself for having taken advantage of her. Enraged at Uriah's mean action, David strikes him on the cheek. Uriah annoys David all the more by forgiving him. A distance comes between Doctor and Annie Strong, to which Mr Dick is very sensitive and sympathetic. David receives a worried letter from Mrs Micawber, reporting her husband's strange and chill behaviour and asking for advice.

NOTES AND GLOSSARY

guava: a fruit
the man in the south ... plum porridge: refers to a nursery rhyme
happily unconscious stranger: Mrs Micawber means a new baby

Chapter 43: Another retrospect

David recalls the passing of time during this happy period of his life. Now he is twenty-one, and has fulfilled his ambition of becoming a parliamentary reporter. He still works occasionally at Doctors' Commons, and has also become an author, writing regularly for magazines. He recalls the elaborate preparations for his marriage to Dora, and the dream-like wedding itself, attended by Traddles, Peggotty, Aunt Betsey,

Dora's aunts, Mr Dick; and with Agnes and Traddles's Sophy as bridesmaids.

NOTES AND GLOSSARY

Britannia ... red tape: David realises that the government is complicated and held up by too many unnecessary procedures and foolish details

a Conveyancer: a lawyer who deals with the transference of property from one person to another

the Stamp Office: the office which issued the stamps which had to be fixed to legal documents

a Masonic understanding: a secret association

Chapter 44: Our housekeeping

David and Dora now have 'no one to please but one another'. They have their first unhappiness together because of Dora's impractical nature. David asks his Aunt Betsey for help in instructing her. She sensibly refuses such a hard-hearted task, reminding him of his own childhood, and of his responsibility for his joint future with Dora. There are more domestic difficulties. They are cheated by tradesmen and troubled by servants. After Traddles has come to a particularly disastrous dinner, Dora excuses herself by asking David to think of her as his 'child-wife'. Difficulties, and Dora's incompetence, continue, but David resigns himself to his responsibility, demands little of Dora, and enjoys her love. Aunt Betsey's warmth towards her continues.

NOTES AND GLOSSARY

Blue Beard: a fairy tale character who murdered his wives

bandbox: a very small cottage, so called because it resembles a small piece of luggage (usually made of cardboard, for millinery)

piquet: a small group of soldiers

charing: working as a servant

capers: bread or biscuits and cheese; it can also mean the pickled buds of a shrub, which is less likely here

debates: parliamentary debates, which David had to report

the Incapables: their inefficient servants

Chapter 45: Mr Dick fulfils my Aunt's predictions

Mrs Markleham, Annie's mother, selfishly interferes in relations between Doctor and Mrs Strong. Mr Dick explains to David how worried he is about them, and that he has decided to help them. One

evening David and his aunt visit the Strongs. Mrs Markleham tells
them that she has just overheard the Doctor making his will. It seems
he has complete trust in his wife, and wants to leave everything to her.
Mr Dick brings Mrs Strong to the Doctor, and David and Aunt Betsey
listen while, with interruptions from her mother, Annie Strong learns
of the doubts Heep cast upon her, affirms that she married the Doctor
for love, not money, and says that she never cared for or encouraged
Jack Maldon. She confirms the truth of her love, and explains how she
was silent about Jack Maldon in order to spare her husband's feelings.
She and her husband are entirely reconciled. But some of the words
Annie has used continue to resound uneasily in David's mind.

NOTES AND GLOSSARY

a rubber:	a game of cards, usually whist
Doctor Johnson:	Samuel Johnson (1709-84) the author, who compiled a famous English dictionary
Marplot:	an interfering nuisance, from the character Sir Martin Marplot in Mrs Centlivre's *The Busybody* (1709)

Chapter 46: Intelligence

About a year after his marriage, David happens to walk past Mrs
Steerforth's house and is asked to come in and speak to Rosa Dartle.
Littimer is there, and tells what has happened to Emily and Steerforth
since they ran away from Yarmouth. They travelled widely, but as
Emily grew more dispirited, Steerforth tired of her and left her.
Maddened, Emily ran away, but Littimer does not know where. He has
broken with Steerforth, who is now sailing round Spain. David also
meets Mrs Steerforth. She and Rosa have let him hear this news only
so he may help them in stopping Emily from tempting Steerforth again.
David passes on all this information to Mr Peggotty, who is now most
often in London, and suggests they should find Martha Endell and ask
for her help in finding Emily in London. They find Martha near
Blackfriars Bridge, and follow her into quieter streets.

NOTES AND GLOSSARY

fleet water:	shallow water

Chapter 47: Martha

David and Mr Peggotty follow Martha to a lonely, dirty area on the
bank of the river, where she stands staring at the gloomy water. They
speak to her, assuring her she is not blamed at all for Emily's flight
with Steerforth. They ask for her help in their search for Emily and

Martha agrees, glad to have a good purpose which, she says, will 'save me from the river'. On his way home, David sees in his Aunt Betsey's garden the same strange man they met once before in London. She gives this man money and asks him to go away. When he has gone, she explains to David that this was her husband, and how bitterly he disappointed her. She asks David to keep all this secret.

NOTES AND GLOSSARY
the life of an owl: a life only at night
made ducks and drakes of: spent foolishly

Chapter 48: Domestic

Now a successful author, David gives up his job as a parliamentary reporter. After a year and a half of marriage, domestic difficulties continue, and, following a particularly unpleasant episode with a page boy, David speaks to Dora again. She is as unreasonable as before. He tries to 'form her mind' to his own satisfaction, but, realising it is already formed, decides he must love her for herself, as she is. Yet he still vaguely experiences a sense of loss and incompleteness in his life. Dora fails to have a child, and remains weak and ill afterwards. Sadly, David realises her condition is serious. Even her dog Jip is frail and ageing.

NOTES AND GLOSSARY
a perfect Whittington ... Lord Mayor: in the traditional story, Dick Whittington ran away from London with his pet cat, but, hearing a prophecy of his future success, returned and became Lord Mayor of London
like scarlet beans: scarlet beans grow very quickly
transported: transportation to Australia was an alternative punishment to imprisonment
a fife: a sort of flute

Chapter 49: I am involved in mystery

David receives from Mr Micawber another of his elaborate and despairing letters, suggesting David and Traddles meet him when he comes to London. Traddles has received a worrying letter from Mrs Micawber, telling of her husband's strange and unpleasant behaviour, and asking for help. Traddles and David meet Micawber, and together they go to Aunt Betsey's house, where Mr Dick tries hard to console Mr Micawber, who is confused and very upset about something. Too worried even to make punch, he can restrain himself no longer, and suddenly begins a violent accusation of Uriah Heep, his employer. He leaves, mysteriously arranging a meeting in Canterbury in a week's time, and confirming this by letter.

NOTES AND GLOSSARY

D.V.:   deo volente (*Latin*), God willing

the D.:   the devil

in esse: (*Latin*) who is now

in posse: (*Latin*) who may be in the future

our coarser national sports: boxing

a mountebank: a showman and performer of tricks for money

the devouring element: fire

Taboo: (*Polynesian*) a restriction or prohibition

Mount Vesuvius: a volcano

the Immortal Exciseman: the poet Robert Burns. (See notes on Chapter 28)

Each in his narrow cell . . . sleep: Micawber quotes Gray's *Elegy written in a Country Churchyard* (1750)

Chapter 50: Mr Peggotty's dream comes true

Mr Peggotty still firmly believes Emily is alive. One day Martha warns him not to leave London. Some time later, having left a note for Mr Peggotty, she hurriedly finds David and takes him to her room. Rosa Dartle is there first, and from the next room they hear her scornfully and bitterly remind Emily of her shame and misery, and threaten her with public disgrace. David does not interfere, as he feels Mr Peggotty should be the first to see Emily. Just as Rosa is leaving, Mr Peggotty arrives at last, and he and Emily are dramatically and tenderly reunited.

Chapter 51: The beginning of a longer journey

The morning after finding Emily, Mr Peggotty tells David and Aunt Betsey her story. After Steerforth left her, she fled from Littimer. Confused and fevered, she was cared for by a young woman, recovered, sailed to France, and then came to London, where Martha rescued her from 'worse than death'. Now Emily, reconciled with her uncle, is safe at his lodgings. He has decided they will go to Australia in six weeks' time and begin a new life there. First Mr Peggotty returns to Yarmouth with David, who finds Mr Omer in poorer health, but still cheerful and interested to hear about Martha and Emily. David goes on to visit Peggotty, Ham, and Mrs Gummidge. Ham asks David to pass on to Emily his generous and forgiving feelings, and his gratitude to Mr Peggotty. Mrs Gummidge begs Mr Peggotty to take her with him and Emily to Australia, where she promises to make herself useful. When

Mr Peggotty leaves Yarmouth, and the old boat-house, now empty and deserted, she happily goes along with him. David also returns to London.

NOTES AND GLOSSARY

pervising: (*dialect*) providing

clicketten: (*dialect*) talking

the dust ... blessed hand: a reference to the Bible story of the woman taken in adultery, whom Jesus forgave; John 8

Sermuchser: (*dialect*) so much so

wheer neither moth ... corrupt; wheer the wicked ... at rest: heaven. See the Bible, Matthew 6 and Job 3

speeches of go-cart: species of pram or push-chair

Chapter 52: I assist at an explosion

Agreeing to leave Dora briefly, David and Aunt Betsey go to Canterbury with Traddles and Mr Dick. Mr Micawber meets them at the hotel, as arranged, and they follow him to Wickfield and Heep's office, where they meet Uriah, and Agnes. Despite Uriah's nasty threats and his mother's pleading, Micawber grandly and dramatically reads out a list of Heep's forgeries, thefts, and many crimes against Mr Wickfield. Aunt Betsey realises the money she lost was taken by Heep. She invented the story of its loss in poor investments to protect Wickfield. Threatening him with the law, and prison, Traddles forces Heep to hand over all the firm's books and accounts, and to remain in his room. Mr Dick, Aunt Betsey, and David watch Mr Micawber (now at ease after his great exposure of Heep) return to his family, to their great mutual joy. Aunt Betsey suggests the Micawbers, with financial help, might also emigrate to Australia. They seem enthusiastic

NOTES AND GLOSSARY

stipendiary: employee

playing Booty: plotting together nastily against one individual

the Gaul ... Bureau: *bureau* is French for office

the philosophic Dane: Hamlet; 'worse remains behind' is quoted from Shakespeare, *Hamlet,* Act III Scene 4

trust-money: money given to the firm for investment

chicaneries: trickery, cheating

the Venerable Pile: Canterbury Cathedral

Chapter 53: Another retrospect

David sadly recalls the time of Dora's illness. She is cheerful, but weakens, and now always remains in bed. David comes to realise she is dying. Dora tells him that she has been very happy, but that her death is for the best, as David would have tired of his child-wife. Now Dora asks to see Agnes, who has come at her request. While David regretfully thinks over his marriage, Jip, old and weak, lies down and dies. Agnes enters weeping, one arm upraised, and David knows Dora is dead too.

NOTES AND GLOSSARY
Who wept: Christ

Chapter 54: Mr Micawber's transactions

It is decided that David ought to go abroad. First, he returns to Canterbury with Aunt Betsey. Traddles and Micawber have energetically investigated the affairs of Wickfield and Heep, and Traddles reports that Mr Wickfield, befriended by Mr Dick and improved in health, is clear of debt. Agnes decides he should stop work. She will support him by keeping a school. Aunt Betsey's money has been recovered from Heep, who has gone with his mother to London. The Micawbers have decided to go to Australia, and have been preparing for the farming life. Mrs Micawber hopes her family will be reconciled with Mr Micawber before their departure. It is arranged that Mr Micawber's debts to Heep will be paid, and he will be given a loan to help him to start anew. After their return to London, David realises what has been troubling his aunt when he goes with her to the funeral of her husband. Micawber describes in yet another letter his arrest for debt and release when Traddles paid it.

NOTES AND GLOSSARY
incubus: an evil spirit
Consols: Government securities
'Now's the day ... slavery': another quotation from Burns

Chapter 55: Tempest

David passes on to Emily by letter the message for her which Ham gave him. He receives a reply for Ham, and, restless himself, takes it to Yarmouth personally. On the way, a terrible storm begins. At Yarmouth, a great wind has made the sea a chaos of vast waves. Ham is absent, but is expected to return the following morning. The storm continues violently all night. After broken sleep, David is called to the shore to see a wreck nearby. Most of the wrecked ship's crew are swept into the sea: eventually only one very active man remains. David thinks he seems strangely familiar. Suddenly Ham appears, determined to attempt a rescue by taking a rope to the ship. David tries unsuccessfully to hold him back. Just as Ham reaches the wreck, a huge wave destroys it completely, and batters him. He is pulled ashore, dead. Another body comes to the shore, and David recognises the familiar figure of his old friend: Steerforth.

NOTES AND GLOSSARY
blew great guns: blew very strongly
roads: sheltered water near the shore

Chapter 56: The new wound, and the old

David takes Steerforth's body to Highgate and breaks the news of his death to Rosa Dartle and Mrs Steerforth. Rosa wildly accuses Mrs Steerforth of having spoiled and ruined her son by a bad upbringing, and claims she loved him more and better than his mother ever did. Moaning, Mrs Steerforth collapses into her grief. Rosa cares for her, while David brings the body to the darkened house. To him, 'all the world seemed death and silence'.

Chapter 57: The emigrants

The Micawbers are well prepared for their voyage to Australia. David asks Micawber to help him to keep the news of Ham's death from Mr Peggotty. On their final evening in Britain, Mr Micawber makes more punch to celebrate the departure of the emigrants. David rescues him from another arrest for debt. Mr and Mrs Micawber discuss emigration, and Mr Micawber's prospects. Agnes and Aunt Betsey take their leave. Next day, Peggotty and David say their farewells aboard the crowded ship, at Gravesend. They discover that Mr Peggotty is taking with him Martha Endell as well as Emily and Mrs Gummidge. David has a last glimpse of Emily, and the ship departs.

NOTES AND GLOSSARY
Albion: Britain
Ostade: Adriaen van Ostade (1610–85), a Dutch painter of smoky, crowded, interiors
a windsail: a ventilator
elbow-chairs: chairs with arm rests

Chapter 58: Absence

Lost in many deep griefs, David wanders alone abroad. He settles at last in Switzerland. Soothed by nature and consoled by a letter from Agnes, he starts writing again, and hears of his increasing reputation from visitors. He comes to realise how he loves Agnes, but feels he has lost the chance of spending his life with her, and that he must not risk trying to change their relationship. He is sadly sure that she will never now be his. He returns home after three years.

Chapter 59: Return

Back in London, David goes to find Traddles at Gray's Inn. He worries about his friend's apparent lack of reputation, but is delighted to be reunited with him. He finds Traddles and Sophy are now married at last, and several of her sisters are living with them. Traddles explains how his marriage took place, and David witnesses his domestic happiness. By chance, he meets Mr Chillip, the doctor, and hears from him that Mr Murdstone continues as before, making his new wife's life miserable, and is still darkly and joylessly religious. David goes on to Dover, and is happily reunited there with Mr Dick, Aunt Betsey (back in her old house), and Peggotty, now her housekeeper.

NOTES AND GLOSSARY
plate: table-ware, cutlery
Westminster Hall: a famous law court in London
cockboat: a very small, frail boat
Britannia metal: a cheap alloy of tin
DOE dem. JIPES versus WIGZELL: a court case
Michaelmas Term: the court session beginning at the end of September
pounce: a powder used to dry ink
wafers: usually thin biscuits, here used to mean a thin piece of paste
negus: wine with hot water, flavoured and sweetened
phrenological development: phrenology was the study of the outside of the skull as an indication of the mental faculties it contained

Chapter 60: Agnes

David hears from his aunt good news of the emigrants, and of Mr Dick and Mr Wickfield. She also tells him that she thinks Agnes is emotionally attached to someone. David goes to Canterbury, where he joyfully finds Agnes as good and beautiful as ever. He spends a pleasant day with her and Mr Wickfield, recalling the past. He tells Agnes how very much he respects and relies on her, and rides back to Dover, still sad that they can never love one another fully.

Chapter 61: I am shown two interesting penitents

David visits London, where Traddles and Sophy continue their great happiness together. Traddles describes their domestic bliss. David has had a letter from his old headmaster, Creakle, now a Middlesex magistrate, inviting him to visit a model prison. David goes with Traddles, and is very suspicious of the prison's system, especially when he finds, to his surprise, that two of the inmates are Heep and Littimer, who seem to take advantage of it very easily. Uriah was imprisoned for a fraud on the Bank of England, and Littimer for robbery. It turns out he was caught by Miss Mowcher.

NOTES AND GLOSSARY

jobbed: acted corruptly

Tower of Babel: an enormous structure, mentioned in the Bible (Genesis 11). The aim of its builders, to reach heaven, was defeated when God confused them by making them all speak different languages

a great many foxes: refers to Aesop's fable 'The Fox and the Grapes', in which the fox says the grapes are sour only because he cannot reach them

a most impious and awful parallel: with Christ

Immaculates: Heep and Littimer

Samson: a strong man, see the Bible, Judges 13–16

Hobby: a Hobby Horse—a foolish or useless idea

Chapter 62: A Light shines on my way

David continues to feel uneasy about Agnes. Aunt Betsey says she thinks Agnes is going to be married. David rides to Canterbury and asks Agnes to share her secret with him. She is upset. At last David understands the clues in her behaviour, and declares to her his long and lasting love. Agnes tells him that she has loved him all her life. This was the secret of her actions. They return together to Dover and delight Aunt Betsey with the news. They are married within a fortnight. Agnes reveals that this wedding was Dora's dying wish.

Chapter 63: A visitor

Ten years after his marriage, when David is famous, rich, and very happy with Agnes, they are visited by Mr Peggotty, who has returned briefly from Australia. From him they hear news of the emigrants. Mr Peggotty himself has been successful as a farmer. He learned of Ham's death, and despite his efforts, Emily eventually heard of it too. She has remained solitary and devoted herself to helping others. Martha Endell has married; Mrs Gummidge violently rejected a proposal. Micawber has become a magistrate, and from an old newspaper, David learns of his highly respected position. Mell, the teacher dismissed from Salem House, is now Doctor Mell, and a headmaster in Micawber's town. Before his return, Mr Peggotty meets his sister again, and Aunt Betsey. He visits Ham's tomb, and takes from it a piece of grass for Emily.

NOTES AND GLOSSARY

grog: rum and water
Non Nobis: (*Latin*) a grace before the meal
votaries of Terpsichore: dancers. Terpsichore was the Greek goddess of the dance
Sol: the sun
'Though seas ... roared': from Burns, *Auld Lang Syne*

Chapter 64: A last retrospect

David gives a last summary of his own life and the lives of those around him. He and Agnes have had several children. Peggotty and Aunt Betsey, older, closer, but otherwise the same, help to look after them. Mr Dick still happily makes kites; Doctor Strong, contented with Annie, continues work on his dictionary. Julia Mills, now married, has returned from India and become a friend of Jack Maldon. Mrs Steerforth, disturbed in her mind, still lives in fretful isolation with Rosa Dartle. Traddles is now a successful lawyer, will soon be a judge, and lives happily in a big house with Sophy and many of her family. Above all, David recalls the light always shed on his life by the presence and influence of his wife, Agnes.

NOTES AND GLOSSARY

Croesus: a very rich man. Croesus was a great king of the sixth century BC, famous for his wealth
Tiffin: a word of Anglo-Indian origin meaning lunch

Part 3

Commentary

A novel of personal memory

What sort of story is *David Copperfield*, and how is it told? We may begin to answer this question by remembering what the title of the novel tells us. Of course, it is usually just called *David Copperfield*, for convenience, but the full original title was *The Personal History, Adventures, Experience, and Observation of David Copperfield, the Younger, of Blunderstone Rookery. (Which He never meant to be Published on any Account)*. Notice how strongly the complete title suggests that this is one man's story of himself, and written for himself. Not only is it a 'Personal History', but it is also supposed 'never ... to be Published on any Account'. Later, (in Chapter 42) this condition is repeated: 'this manuscript is intended for no eyes but mine'. Of course, this is part of the fiction: after all, we are reading David's story ourselves when we reach this sentence. But it remains true that *David Copperfield* is David's private act of looking back over his own life—his 'Adventures, Experience, and Observation'—and of making it into a personal, individual record which he writes himself. So *David Copperfield* is a fictional autobiography: David's recollection of the events and situations through which he grew and developed into the man he has become at the time he writes. It is David Copperfield's own story of his life as he remembers it himself. As David remarks in Chapter 58, 'this narrative is my written memory'.

A 'written memory' is a good summary of the way *David Copperfield* is presented. We are often reminded, in the course of the novel, of the importance of memory and of the way events are recalled. David, in writing his personal memory, is of course not writing about events as they are happening, but remembering things that happened to him long before. Yet many of these happenings still seem very significant to him, and have remained very vivid in his mind. For example, when he is writing about the terrible deaths of Steerforth and Ham in the storm at Yarmouth, he remarks

> I dream of it sometimes ... to this hour. I have an association between it and a stormy wind, or the lightest mention of a sea-shore, as strong as any of which my mind is conscious. As plainly as I behold what happened, I will try to write it down. I do not recall it, but see it done; for it happens again before me. (Chapter 55)

Or, when describing how he once talked to his first love, Dora, he says

The scent of a geranium leaf, at this day, strikes me with a half comical half serious wonder as to what change has come over me in a moment; and then I see a straw hat and blue ribbons, and a quantity of curls, and a little black dog being held up, in two slender arms, against a bank of blossoms and bright leaves. (Chapter 26)

Certain events from David's past life made such a strong impression on him that he still sees them almost as if they were happening again. He often tells particular parts of his past history (such as his mother's funeral, or his marriage to Dora) in the present tense. For example, in describing how Dora died, he writes 'I am again with Dora, in our cottage. I do not know how long she has been ill. I am so used to it in feeling, that I cannot count the time' (Chapter 53), rather than writing, as he does elsewhere, in the past tense, and saying 'I did not know how long she had been ill. I was so used to it in feeling . . .' and so on. Three whole chapters (18, 43, 53) are written in this present tense way. A 'written memory' looks back into the past, but the effect of these passages in the present tense is to show us how David's 'written memory' is a way of making his past present to himself again. *David Copperfield* is the story of a grown-up recalling how he grew up: a mature memory of how maturity was reached. David remembers that his past is part of him still, and that it has made him what he is. His frequent claims that he can still see the past very clearly, and his occasional use of the present tense in describing it, help to show us how important his past is for him, and what it means to him.

Although David has such a strong memory of many of the events in his life that it can seem almost as if they are happening again, it is made clear from the start that the story we are told is written not as it happens, but many years later. In the first few pages of Chapter 1, David tells us what happened long afterwards to the 'caul' he was born with, and also explains how he knows the story. As David has grown up in the world, obviously he has learned a lot more about it than he knew when he was a boy, or a young man. His greater knowledge as he writes, during his later life, affects the way he feels about how he grew up, and his way of telling the story. For example, when he first met Steerforth and Emily, he could not have known that they would later run away together. But he knows, as he writes the story of those first meetings, what did happen later. So he especially mentions, for example, that Emily wanted to be a lady even when she was a little girl. He even says, remembering how Emily risked falling into the sea,

There has been a time since . . . when I have asked myself the question, would it have been better for little Em'ly to have had the waters close above her head that morning in my sight; and when I have answered Yes, it would have been. (Chapter 3)

He recalls, later, how excited little Em'ly looked when she first heard about Steerforth (Chapter 10). There are many more examples of David's way of realising, as he looks back on the past, how significant some parts of it were, although he could not have known this at the time: Ham looking out to sea and thinking of his 'end' (Chapter 32), Aunt Betsey saying 'blind, blind blind!' about David's affection for Dora, and so on. Such suggestions of what might happen later remind us that *David Copperfield* is a 'written memory'. They also keep the reader in suspense and increase interest in what will happen next in the novel.

When he writes about his boyhood, David admits that he allows his 'later understanding' to come to his aid. As a result, he can look back on his childhood with a special humour, anger, or insight, because he understands later much more about what he experienced at the time. For example, when David writes about how Murdstone called him 'Brooks of Sheffield' (Chapter 2), or how he once thought the eldest Miss Larkins was the most wonderful girl in the world, it amuses him—and us—to look back upon how young and easily fooled he was. He can also remember, sadly, how firmly he believed in Steerforth, or in Dora, and how mistaken he later discovered he had been.

Dickens's sympathy for children, and his understanding of them, always helped him to imagine their lives very convincingly. The first few chapters of *David Copperfield* are often said to be the best in the novel. David's childhood seems very true to life, and a special feeling is added by the way David remembers it when he is older and wiser. He often uses his later thoughts to comment upon his younger life, and looks back upon it with nostalgia; that is, with a sad warmth which remembers how it was and also feels regret that it has passed. Perhaps one reason *David Copperfield* has always been such a popular novel is that it reminds us so effectively how we sometimes feel when we recall our own childhoods—'The days sported by us, as if Time had not grown up himself yet, but were a child too, and always at play' (Chapter 3).

David Copperfield's method of presenting his own life history succeeds not only because he obviously knows his own story very well, but also because he is a very good storyteller. This is clear from the fact that he becomes a famous novelist later in life. It is also obvious from his manner of telling his own story. David was a very observant and highly imaginative child, and he has retained these talents all his life:

I believe the power of observation in numbers of very young children to be quite wonderful for its closeness and accuracy ... if it should appear from anything I may have set down in this narrative that I was a child of close observation, or that as a man I have a strong memory of my childhood, I undoubtedly lay claim to both of these characteristics. (Chapter 2)

Not only was David very observant, but he retained a child's talent for fanciful imagination. For example, the following passages record his impression of Barkis's horse, and of Mr Mell playing his flute:

> The carrier's horse was the laziest horse in the world, I should hope, and shuffled along, with his head down, as if he liked to keep people waiting to whom packages were directed. I fancied, indeed, that he sometimes chuckled audibly over this reflection, but the carrier said he was only troubled with a cough. (Chapter 3)

> He took out his flute, and blew at it, until I almost thought he would gradually blow his whole being into the large hole at the top, and ooze away at the keys. (Chapter 7)

David's 'fancy' and 'almost thoughts' create very striking descriptions. There are many more examples: how he thinks the birds should peck Peggotty's red arms instead of apples (Chapter 2), or thinks the dead may rise up from their graves in the churchyard (Chapter 2), and so on. He puts this powerful imagination to good use when he tells Steerforth stories at school:'whatever I had within me that was romantic and dreamy, was encouraged by so much story-telling in the dark' (Chapter 7). David also amuses himself, during his unhappy time in London, by making up stories about the people and situations he sees there. He remembers this later:

> When my thoughts go back, now, to that slow agony of my youth, I wonder how much of the histories I invented for such people hangs like a mist of fancy over well-remembered facts! When I tread the old ground, I do not wonder that I seem to see and pity, going on before me, an innocent romantic boy, making his imaginative world out of such strange experiences and sordid things! (Chapter 11)

David's talent for imagination, and for story-telling, do indeed spread 'a mist of fancy over well-remembered facts', and make his 'written memory' vivid and entertaining. He is a successful narrator of his own history: his story is an 'imaginative world' he has made not only out of 'strange experiences and sordid things' but out of all his experience of his own life.

There are many ways of telling a story, and the author's choice of method usually decides what sort of novel we will read. In most novels, the narrator tells the story of other people, in the third person (he, she, they). Novels like *David Copperfield*, in which one of the people in the story is also the person who is supposed to be telling it, are said to be written in the first person: that is, the narrator writes about 'what I did', 'what happened to me', and so on.

Structure and plot

Main Story

The structure of *David Copperfield* is simple, as a result of the nature of the novel. Since it is a novel of autobiography, in which David recalls his past life, the story starts with his birth and continues straight forward until the moment of his writing. He follows his development up to that point, recording the influence of his experience and of the people with whom he came into contact. The progress of David's life connects the events of the novel, and gives it coherence. Dickens's biographer, John Forster, remarked of *David Copperfield*

'That the incidents arise easily, and to the very end connect themselves naturally and unobtrusively with the characters of which they are a part, is to be said perhaps more truly of this than of any other of Dickens's novels. There is a profusion of distinct and distinguished people, and a prodigal wealth of detail; but the unity of drift or purpose is apparent always, and the tone is uniformly right.'*

David's story of his life is completely central to the novel. It falls into three main parts:

(1) his childhood and early youth, starting with his birth in Blunderstone and ending when he completes his time at Doctor Strong's school in Canterbury. (Chapters 1–18)

(2) his later youth and early manhood, starting with him 'looking about' for a career and ending with the death of his first wife, Dora. (Chapters 19–53)

(3) his maturity, starting from his mourning for Dora (and Steerforth and Ham) and ending with his marriage to Agnes Wickfield and happy life afterwards. (Chapters 54–64)

Notice how each part of the story of his life ends with one of the 'Retrospect' chapters (18, 53, 64), which quickly and briefly summarise events which happened over a long period of time.

This division of the novel into sections is intended only as a rough guide. Within each part, other useful divisions could be made, and crises occur: for example, his marriage to Dora, or Aunt Betsey's announcement that she has lost all her money, each start a whole new sort of life for David.

Sub-plots

Along with the central story of David's own life, several other secondary stories are told. The two most substantial of these sub-plots are the

*John Forster, *The Life of Charles Dickens*, p.554.

stories of (1) Uriah Heep, Wickfield, and eventually Mr Micawber; and (2) Steerforth, Emily, and the Peggotty family. The story of Heep, Micawber, and Wickfield reaches its climax in Chapter 52, 'I assist at an Explosion'; the Emily, Steerforth, and Mr Peggotty story slightly later, in Chapter 55, 'Tempest'. The two stories balance one another. The Heep story has a happy ending: Mr Wickfield recovers; Uriah Heep, the villain, is exposed and defeated; and everybody's fortune is restored. Steerforth's story ends tragically: although Mr Peggotty recovers Emily (Chapter 50), Steerforth (whom David never thought of as a villain, anyway) is drowned, and the innocent Ham dies along with him.

There are other less substantial sub-plots: the story of Aunt Betsey and her husband; the story of Doctor and Annie Strong and Jack Maldon; and the adventures of the Micawber family. Of course, David is connected with the events of all of these stories, as he knows all the people who figure in each. And the events of the sub-plots often involve him directly; for example, it is through Uriah's evil plans that Aunt Betsey seems to lose all her money, leaving David to look after himself. David is also directly responsible for introducing Steerforth to Emily in the first place.

All the secondary stories are intricately bound up with David's own life, and each adds significance to it. Without his involvement with the Micawbers, Steerforth, Mr Peggotty, and so on, his life would be uneventful and incomplete. But although the sub-plots are relevant to David's own story, they do remain secondary to it. In particular, David as narrator can record only those events he witnesses himself. Most of the happenings of the sub-plots take place beyond his direct knowledge, and so have to be told by someone else. For example, Mr Micawber reads out an explanation of all Uriah Heep's crimes; and David has to learn about what happens to Steerforth and Emily first from Littimer and later from Mr Peggotty.

David Copperfield is a carefully constructed novel. David's own story, and all the sub-plots, are arranged together to form a very well-organised whole. Dickens once wanted to use separately the stories of Dora, and of little Em'ly, for one of his public readings. But he remarked in a letter

> 'There is still the huge difficulty that I constructed the whole with immense pains, and have so woven it up and blended it together, that I cannot yet so separate the parts as to tell the story of David's married life with Dora, and the story of Mr Peggotty's search for his niece.'*

*Charles Dickens, *The Letters of Charles Dickens* ed. Walter Dexter, The Nonesuch Press, London, 1938, Vol.II, p.619.

Coincidence

It is true that the main story and all the sub-plots of *David Copperfield* are 'woven up and blended together', but it might seem to a modern reader that Dickens uses too many coincidences in bringing together characters from the different stories. There certainly are very many extraordinary coincidences in *David Copperfield*. Here are some examples: Mr Micawber happens to be passing the Heeps' house in Canterbury, and sees David inside. Later, David discovers his old schoolfriend Traddles is now the Micawbers' lodger. Jane Murdstone turns up again as Dora's companion. Agnes happens to be in the theatre the very night David is so drunk. Dora and Jip die at the same moment. Steerforth's ship happens to be sailing past Yarmouth when it is wrecked, Ham dies trying to save him, and David chances to be there at the time. These are only a few examples. There are very many more throughout *David Copperfield*. There are also some other happenings which might seem unlikely. For example, it seems strange that both the Micawbers and Mr Peggotty decide so suddenly to go off to Australia. And their great success there, and the happiness of almost everyone at the end of the novel, may seem 'too good to be true'.

Such episodes, and the presence of so many coincidences, sometimes makes the story seem unrealistic, as though it could never have happened in the real world of everyday life. But this is not necessarily a serious fault in the novel, or a mistake on Dickens's part. Dickens, like Smollett and Fielding before him, was more interested in showing the nature of character than in creating a convincing plot. (see p.11) Dickens's first readers probably accepted coincidences in a story more easily than we do today. And *David Copperfield* is constructed to show the characters, David particularly, as clearly as possible.

Serialisation

The fact that Dickens first published *David Copperfield* in the form of a serial of twenty monthly parts influenced the way he wrote the novel, and partly affected its structure. What effects might be expected from this method of writing a novel in successive pieces, instead of all at once? Such effects can be summarised as follows. (Only numbers 4 and 5 affect structure.)

(1) *Popularity.* Dickens could follow the sales figures for each monthly part, so he always knew how well the public liked his work. This encouraged him to seek popularity and write for a large public.

(2) *Topicality.* Dickens could include in his story things which were in the news at the time.

(3) *Reminders.* As its parts appeared only once a month, the whole

novel took one and a half years to read. There was a risk of readers forgetting who characters were. Dickens probably hoped to avoid this risk by using various ways of making his characters very distinctive and memorable. (See notes on Character, p.58.)

(4) *Suspense.* If readers did not want to find out how the story continued, they simply wouldn't buy the next part of the novel when it appeared. So Dickens usually ended each part with something exciting or mysterious, or a suggestion of what might happen in the future, so that readers would want to know what happened next.

(5) Difficulties. There are obvious difficulties for an author in the method of serial publication. Firstly, Dickens had to remind his readers from time to time of what was happening in each of the various sub-plots. Secondly, Dickens actually wrote the parts of the story every month, often quite shortly before they were published. So when he began *David Copperfield*, Dickens did not know exactly how it would end, and he could not go back and change previous episodes as he wrote, because these had already been published.

Dickens largely overcame these difficulties. The stories of *David Copperfield* are 'woven up and blended together' so that nothing is forgotten. Characters from each part of the story appear regularly. And although Dickens may not have known exactly how his story would end, he must have had a close idea, for the events of the first chapters look ahead to what is to follow. It was pointed out (see p.47) that the reader is kept in suspense by many hints of what may happen much later in the story. Dickens could not have written such passages without knowing how his story would continue.

Dickens overcame the problems of serialisation with a carefully constructed story. His only serious difficulty occurred when he copied Miss Mowcher from a real dwarf whom he knew. She complained to him, and Dickens was forced to promise that he would change her character in a later episode. So a strange change seems to take place between Miss Mowcher's first appearance in Chapter 22 and her much more pleasant manner in Chapter 32.

Style

Description, realism, and imagination

Dickens was often called 'the Inimitable', and his style of writing is certainly unique. He was a careful and accurate observer, and success-fully presents scenes visually. Descriptions are always very full of detail: remember for example how Mr Peggotty's house is described (Chapter 3). In certain scenes, these details build up until a complete, powerful, and elaborate impression is formed. (For example, look at Chapter 47, the description of the gloomy area by the river where Martha Endell is found by David and Mr Peggotty.) This is especially true of the famous description of the storm (Chapter 55), in which all the details—the sand and seaweed blowing through the streets, the great waves, people struggling to walk about, the huge sheets of lead blown off roofs—all add up to give a thorough impression of the tremendous wind.

Likewise, Dickens presents characters' appearances carefully and elaborately, and with an eye for significant detail. For example, remember David's first sight of Mr Micawber:

A stoutish, middle-aged person, in a brown surtout and black tights and shoes, with no more hair upon his head (which was a large one, and very shining) than there is upon an egg, and with a very extensive face ... His clothes were shabby, but he had an imposing shirt-collar on. He carried a jaunty sort of a stick, with a large pair of rusty tassles to it; and a quizzing-glass hung outside his coat—for ornament, I afterwards found, as he very seldom looked through it, and couldn't see anything when he did. (Chapter 11)

This description helps us to visualise Mr Micawber clearly, but it does more than that. It tells us a lot about him. His clothes are shabby, but also rather stylish. His stick has rusty tassles, but it is a jaunty stick. Mr Micawber's appearance already suggests something of his poverty, and of the constant jaunty hopefulness with which he resists it. The useless eye-glass also indicates that there is something strange or amusing about this man.

Of course, not all characters are described at quite such length. But even when the description seems casual—for example, David's first notice of Murdstone's rather gloomy 'shallow black eye' and thick, dark whiskers (Chapter 2)—there is usually a suggestion of the nature of the person described. Dickens's detailed visual descriptions are full of suggestion.

Dickens's description is so visually detailed, and seems so careful and accurate, that it has often been called superb realism, showing life just as it is. But this is not exactly true, for Dickens is much more than a realist. His great interest in experience and people creates close attention to the commonest episode or object, but the basic characteristic of his style is exaggeration. He presents not a normal reality, but a reality heightened, sharpened and brightened by the exercise of his energetic imagination. Dickens's novels are enlivened by his enormous imaginative vitality, which makes both characters and descriptions vivid and intense. George Orwell, the English novelist and critic, said of Dickens that 'His imagination overwhelms everything, like a kind of weed'.* This

*George Orwell, *Collected Essays*, Secker and Warburg, London, 1961. p.77.

suggests something excessive about his style, and it is true that Dickens does seem to be carried away at times by his 'overwhelming' imagination. In describing a scene or person, he sometimes invents something striking but unlikely, and then makes it true. For example, the following description of Doctor Strong:

> He would have taken his gaiters off his legs, to give away. In fact, there was a story current among us (I have no idea, and never had, on what authority, but I have believed it for so many years I feel quite certain it is true), that one frosty day, one winter-time, he actually did bestow his gaiters on a beggar-woman . . . (Chapter 16)

There follows a story of the Doctor's gaiters.

Some critics suggest that Dickens goes too far in this way; that his descriptions are unnecessarily detailed, and his characters too elaborate, and impossible. But most of his readers appreciate his effective mixture of the real with the fanciful. Just as Mr Micawber's 'epistolary powers, in describing this unfortunate state of things, really seemed to outweigh any pain or anxiety that the reality could have caused him' (Chapter 52), so Dickens's imaginative powers outweigh reality and spiritedly create a new, fabulous world of his own. It is a world in which buttons explode from Peggotty's gown whenever she is upset, Mr Micawber passes from joy to misery in minutes, a donkey can send shivers down Betsey Trotwood's spine, Uriah's clammy hand leaves slimy trails on the page he reads, and so on: it is a fantastic world. Through it all, David as narrator overwhelms fact with the mists of his fancy. This produces many strange and effective descriptions, which often turn scenes into stories:

> A very old house bulging out over the road; a house with long low lattice windows bulging out still farther, and beams with carved heads on the ends bulging out too, so that I fancied the whole house was leaning forward, trying to see who was passing on the narrow pavement below. (Chapter 15)

> The master of this shop was sitting at the door in his shirt-sleeves, smoking; and as there were a great many coats and pairs of trousers dangling from the low ceiling, and only two feeble candles burning inside to show what they were, I fancied that he looked like a man of revengeful disposition, who had hung all his enemies, and was enjoying himself. (Chapter 13)

Scenes and characters are more strikingly 'life-like' than real life itself, and this is what makes so many of them unforgettable. Even unimportant characters are given some memorable feature: for example, 'Mr Larkins (a gruff old gentleman with a double chin, and one of his eyes immoveable in his head)' (Chapter 18); or 'A half-dressed boatman, standing next me, pointed with his bare arm (a tattoo'd arrow on it, pointing in the same direction)' (Chapter 55).

Prose

Dickens's language is for the most part quite straightforward and easy, perhaps especially when David is recalling his simple early childhood. His prose gets a little more complicated as his life goes on. Although the language is mostly quite direct, it is also varied. *David Copperfield* is a very long novel, but it does not seem monotonous. The prose is simple, but Dickens includes in it many flourishes: David's narration, like Mr Micawber's speech, often contains grand or elaborate ways of saying something quite simple. David writes, for example that he 'would hear of no such immolation on the altar of friendship', when he means only that he would not let Traddles eat raw meat (Chapter 44). The prose is energetic and inventive in its constant verbal wit and use of amusing phrases. It is also enlivened by the frequent use of simile. As mentioned already, David, the imaginative child, very often makes interesting and unusual comparisons, seeing things happening 'as if . . .' or 'fancying that . . .'

David Copperfield contains an unusually great amount of direct speech. Dickens's characters' appearances are carefully noted, but they also have a lot to say for themselves, and about themselves. They are certainly heard as well as seen. And Dickens very often uses a character's manner of speaking, as well as what he says, as a way of making him individual, distinct, and memorable. The best example of this is, of course, Mr Micawber's exaggerated and ridiculous eloquence, but several other characters have a very distinct manner of speech: Barkis has little to say, Betsey Trotwood is abrupt and direct, and Ham and Mr Peggotty talk partly in dialect, the local speech of Yarmouth. The use of so much direct speech, and of such different kinds, helps to add variety to the language of *David Copperfield*, and to retain the reader's interest.

Humour

David Copperfield is one of Dickens's most entertaining novels. Humour is constantly a part of the imaginative energy of Dickens's style of writing, and verbal wit is a characteristic of his prose.

What makes us laugh? Humour is never easy to discuss, and harder still to define, but we can recognise one or two different ways Dickens uses the comic in *David Copperfield*.

(1) *Humour of Personality.* Some of the most memorable comic characters in English literature appear in *David Copperfield*. Mr Micawber

(his constant hopefulness that 'something will turn up'; his grand speech; his changeable joys and sorrows), Betsey Trotwood (chasing donkeys; or constantly afraid of fire in London), Mr Dick (always worried about King Charles's head), are all highly eccentric, and amusing in themselves because they act so strangely. Many other less eccentric characters also behave with laughable strangeness: Mrs Crupp with her 'spazzums'; Mr Chillup, constantly timid and fearful; Barkis, kindly but 'a little near' about money; Mr Omer, cheerful even when confined to his chair; Mr Spenlow, pretending to be afraid of his partner Jorkins; and so on.

(2) *Humour of Situation.* There are many episodes in *David Copperfield* which are funny in themselves. Often these have to do with David's inexperience or his position as a child in an adult world. The 'Brooks of Sheffield' incident has already been mentioned, but there are other times when David is confused or cheated, for example by the waiter, William, in the inn at Yarmouth when he is on his way to school. Such situations are often presented ironically: that is, David (as he writes) and the reader know more of his situation than he knew at the time. For example, David remarks during the 'Brooks of Sheffield' incident 'In short, we quite enjoyed ourselves'; and finds William the waiter 'So very friendly and companionable', when in fact we know that the reverse was truly the case. Irony—this way of indicating the true meaning by stating its opposite—is often used in *David Copperfield* as David looks back over his past life and realises how silly he sometimes was, and how often his experience was not really as he thought it at the time.

(3) *Dialogue.* The fact that many characters have a distinct manner of speech is often a source of humour. Mr Micawber's wonderful eloquence, or Aunt Betsey's abrupt way of speaking her mind, are good examples of this. The eccentricity of various characters, and their habits of speech, lead to some very amusing exchanges in *David Copperfield*:

' "She was quite overcome, I am afraid," said Mr Dick, with great commiseration.
"What! Did you ever see a crocodile overcome?" inquired my aunt.
"I don't think I ever saw a crocodile," returned Mr Dick, mildly.'
(Chapter 45)

' "Mr Micawber, I wonder you have never turned your thoughts to emigration."
"Madam," returned Mr. Micawber, "it was the dream of my youth, and the fallacious aspiration of my riper years." I am thoroughly persuaded, by the by, that he had never thought of it in his life.'
(Chapter 52)

Dickens's humour is part of his sympathy for his characters, and helps the reader to an understanding of them. They may seem strange or absurd, but Dickens's constant humour in presenting them makes them human. In laughing at them, we may sometimes be enjoying laughing at ourselves.

Pathos

Dickens wants to make his readers laugh, but he is sometimes criticised for also being determined to make them cry. Many of his novels are said to be much too sentimental, spoiled by artificial pathos which many modern readers find unacceptable, or embarrassing. *David Copperfield* is certainly very full of tears. For example, during Mr Peggotty's narration of Emily's story, in Chapter 51, weeping is almost constant, and it is very frequent elsewhere in the novel. Sometimes this seems too much, and certain episodes appear emotionally overdone. Dickens sometimes seems to try unnecessarily to increase a sadness which readers might feel in any case. As a result, he makes emotions exaggerated and false. While we are grateful for Dickens's humour, we sometimes resent the way he interferes with our more tender emotions. For example, when Dora's dog Jip dies at exactly the moment she dies herself (Chapter 53), we may feel this is not just an odd coincidence but a clumsy attempt by Dickens to make us sadder.

But such passages are much more frequent in several of Dickens's other novels than in *David Copperfield*, whose form as David's 'written memory' helps place and control strong emotions. In several passages, such as the description of Barkis's death (Chapter 31), or the last paragraphs of some of the chapters about David's childhood (1, 8, 9, 10, 13, for example), there is a quiet, thoughtful quality which makes emotions seem strong and genuine. It is worth remembering, too, that Dickens's pathos would have seemed much less unusual or unnecessary to his original readers. In fact, it was part of his popularity, for elaborate sentimentality was frequent in Victorian fiction.

Characterisation

General Points

Dickens's warm concern for humanity made character a central interest of his work. His characters are the best and most memorable part of his novels.

Some literary critics, however, do not agree about how good Dickens's characters really are. The novelist E.M. Forster, for example, said that 'Dickens's people are nearly all flat.'* Forster used Mrs Micawber as an example of what he meant by 'flat': 'The really flat character can

*E.M. Forster, *Aspects of the Novel* (1927), Penguin Books, Harmondsworth, 1962, pp.78–9.

be expressed in one sentence such as "I never will desert Mr Micawber." There is Mrs Micawber—she says she won't desert Mr Micawber; she doesn't, and there she is'.* Forster's criticism is really only a version of the most frequent objection to Dickens's characters: that they are not 'real people' but 'caricatures'. That is, they are seen only from the outside, and only one aspect of their appearance or actions is presented, and in a very exaggerated way.

This criticism does suggest something true about Dickens's way of creating characters. Very many of his people are shown doing or saying only one thing, or have one very noticeable feature. As well as Mrs Micawber, consider the following examples from *David Copperfield*. Traddles is always drawing skeletons, or seen with his unruly hair standing on end. Barkis always says 'Barkis is willin'', and he always is. Mr Spenlow worries repeatedly about Mr Jorkins; Doctor Strong about his dictionary. Rosa Dartle's scar is mentioned every time she appears. Mrs Crupp constantly reminds David 'I'm a mother myself'; Mrs Gummidge can't forget that she is 'a lone lorn creetur' ... and everythink goes contrairy'. Dora never appears without her dog Jip, nor Peggotty without her bit of wax-candle.

But Dickens's characters' exaggerated features or repeated words are very noticeable: like labels, they make each one individual and very easily recognisable. It was suggested before (see notes on Style) that Dickens's energetic imagination made him exaggerate everything, made him more than realistic, and his method of characterisation is also a result of this. Although it does make his characters seem unusual, it also makes them unusually memorable, and memorable rather as people we know are remembered in real life—often by only one or two characteristic gestures or sayings.

And it is not really fair to say that Dickens's method shows only the outside of his characters. Rosa Dartle's scar, for example, very accurately indicates her changing moods, and Traddles's skeletons remind us of the problems his cheerfulness always hides. Like appearances (see p.53), characteristics show us a lot about inner natures. Also, Dickens's frequent use of direct speech allows characters to tell us a lot about what they are thinking and who they are. Much of what we know about them is learned directly from what they say themselves.

Criticisms like Forster's do tell us something about Dickens's method of characterisation, but do not necessarily show that there is anything wrong with it. Even Forster admits in the end that there is a 'wonderful feeling of human depth'† to Dickens's characters. His method may seem exaggerated, or unrealistic, but it is often very effective, and it is part of his unique style.

*E.M. Forster, *Aspects of the Novel*, p.75.
†Ibid., p. 74.

A more serious criticism of Dickens is that many of his major characters seem unconvincing, and are presented less successfully than minor figures. In *David Copperfield*, this criticism is made especially of Agnes, and even of David himself.

David Copperfield

The development of David's character is absolutely central to *David Copperfield*, and this will be discussed in the next section (Theme and Unity). However, several criticisms have been made of the way in which Dickens presents this character. For example, it is often said that David's childhood is presented vividly and clearly, but that when the action gets more complicated (after Chapter 18), he 'fades out', becoming a somewhat uninteresting observer, who merely records what happens. This may be partially true: certainly the scenes of David's boyhood are among the best imagined in the novel. But one of the ways in which we know David later is through his reactions to the many other people he meets in his life, and through his way of telling his story. As the action gets more complicated, we learn more about David, too, although often less directly than at first.

Mr Micawber

'A thoroughly good-natured man, and as active a creature about everything but his own affairs as ever existed, and never so happy as when he was busy about something that could never be of any profit to him.' (Chapter 11)

He is a great comic character. Mr Micawber's weakness is that he has a large family but never has any money. His strength is that he never allows this fact to depress or overwhelm him for very long. Although his moods change from joy to misery often, and very quickly, he always recovers his spirits just as rapidly. Sociable and cheerful, he has a great, spirited hopefulness that 'something will turn up', and a carefree manner when it doesn't. Despite his difficulties, he keeps up an impressive appearance. His wonderful talent for speaking and writing letters in elaborate, eloquent language, overcomes Uriah Heep and helps to defeat all his other problems, even the dismal reality of his own life of poverty. Apart from being irresponsible about money ('pecuniary difficulties'), he is a good and loving husband and father. His careful, determined, and selfless exposure of Uriah Heep shows that he càn do something right (apart from making punch), and this prepares us for his later success in Australia. (See chapters 11, 12, 17, 27, 28, 36, 49, 52, 54, and 63).

Uriah Heep

'Always creeping along the ground to some small end or other, he will always magnify every object in the way; and consequently will hate everybody that comes, in the most innocent way, between him and it.' (Chapter 54)

Although constantly saying he is ' 'umble', Uriah hates the society that has forced this pretence on him. He is greedy, very dishonest, and thoroughly nasty. He hates and struggles to hurt or crush anyone, such as David or Mr Wickfield, who is in the way of his ambitions, and even those who are not, such as Doctor Strong. Ruthless and wickedly clever, he will use any means to get what he wants. Uriah is made to seem really sinister and unpleasant by Dickens's very frequent comparison of his disagreeable appearance to damp, slimy creatures: fish, snakes, eels, and snails. However, some sympathy is saved for him when he describes his poor, difficult childhood, when he was forced to learn his ' 'umbleness'. (Chapters 15, 16, 17, 25, 35, 39, 42, 52, 61).

Steerforth

'Ride on! Rough-shod if need be ... Ride on over all obstacles, and win the race!' (Chapter 28)

David greatly admires Steerforth because he seems to have all the social strengths and graces David lacks. Steerforth is charming, handsome, and confident, and seems friendly, generous, and noble. When Steerforth runs off with Emily, David learns what he should have noticed before: his friend is also proud, irresponsible, and selfish. Steerforth has no care at all for the lower orders of society, nor for anyone's feelings except his own. His charm is a deliberately false pretence, used for his own purposes: to trap Emily, and Rosa Dartle before her. As in the case of Uriah Heep, however, Steerforth has suffered from a bad upbringing. His proud mother spoiled him, and he realises himself how badly he lacked the control of 'a judicious father'. (Chapters 6, 7, 19, 20, 21, 22, 24, 28, 29, 55).

Betsey Trotwood

'I have been a grumpy, frumpy, wayward sort of a woman, a good many years. I am still, and I always shall be. But you and I have done one another some good, Trot ...' (Chapter 44)

Severely disappointed and disillusioned by her husband, Aunt Betsey adopts a firm, independent manner of self-reliance, determination, and individuality. The result is a fearless abruptness in speech, a hard and unbending exterior, and 'wonderful self-command'. She stops trusting men, teaches her maids to avoid marriage, and is determined Clara Copperfield's child will be a girl. Disappointed again, she looks after Mr Dick instead. Her appreciation of his child-like, amiable nature prepares for her acceptance of David. Through her generous, loving attachment to him, she softens greatly, and eventually accepts Dora, and Peggotty, completely. Like Peggotty, she becomes a second mother to David.

She remains eccentric all her life, continuing to chase donkeys, ask Mr Dick for his advice, and pace up and down for hours when thinking. She also always remains firm—facing her financial ruin boldly and with determination—but her firmness is more and more transparent as she increasingly has to find excuses for her tears and affection. Although she seems so independent, she is really unselfish: she shields Mr Wickfield, and allows David his own way even when she knows he is wrong. She is a good judge of character, and is delighted by his marriage to Agnes.

Next to David himself, she is the most interesting character in *David Copperfield*, as she develops so clearly. David has to learn that he must discipline his heart; Aunt Betsey learns to discipline her heart less fiercely. (See chapters 1, 13, 14, 15, 23, 34, 35, 44, 47, 52, 62, and 64).

Dora

'Our dearest Dora is a favourite child of nature. She is a thing of light, and airiness, and joy.' (Chapter 37)

Dora Spenlow is beautiful, sweet, attractive and happy, but empty-headed and impractical. She believes in a world where 'ever on any account leaving off dancing, La ra la, La ra la' is an impossibility; where she and her dog Jip can live 'Any how!'. Her pretty sweetness charms David from the moment he first sees her, but he learns, slowly and sadly, why everyone treats her like a child, or a favourite toy. She must always be carefree, and avoids having to think, or act responsibly. When married to David, she is completely unable to look after their house, and unreasonably afraid of any attempt to teach her to improve. She can never understand or follow his advice. She is loving, innocent, and trusting, but never quite the companion that David needs. She excuses herself from his demands by admitting she is impractical and asking him to call her 'child-wife'. When she is dying, she suggests that their marriage could not have continued to be happy. (Chapters 26, 33, 37, 38, 41, 42, 44, 48, 53).

Agnes

'There are goodness, peace and truth wherever Agnes is.' (Chapter 16)

Like Dora, Agnes is beautiful and attractive, but in many ways she is Dora's opposite. Even as a child, she seems quite grown up, and helps look after her father, and his house, whereas Dora never grows up at all. Agnes is calm, reliable, responsible and patient, all qualities Dora lacks. David always asks her for help and advice because she is so sensible, reasonable, and wise. She has an almost saintly goodness, never thinking of herself at all. The secret that Agnes has loved David all her life is only revealed in the end when David realises how long she has been his guide and support, and how his life has always been directed towards her, towards the perfect woman.

Dickens's characterisation of Agnes is often criticised, as she seems too good to be true. As she is so grown up when a child, she has no need to develop, and this makes her seem static and uninteresting. She has every virtue, no obvious faults, and never does anything wrong, but she lacks Dora's vitality, and never seems completely alive to us. (Chapters 15, 25, 35, 39, 52, 53, 60, 62, 64).

Minor Characters

There are so many characters in *David Copperfield* that there is not enough space in these notes to describe each fully. However, E.M. Forster said of Dickens's characters 'Nearly every one can be summed up in a sentence',* and although that is certainly an exaggeration, the following list provides a brief reminder of who's who in *David Copperfield,* and a note of the chapters in which each character appears.

Barkis, the carrier, and Peggotty's husband. 'Barkis is willin'', and 'a good plain creatur''. (Chapters 3, 5, 8, 10, 21, 30, 31).
Mr Chillip, the doctor. 'The meekest of his sex, the mildest of little men.' (Chapters 1, 9, 10, 22, 59).
Clara Copperfield, David's mother. 'Pretty and thoughtless', but affectionate. (Chapters 1–4, 8, 9).
Sophy Crewler, Traddles's fiancée, 'the dearest girl'. (Chapters 27, 34, 43, 59, 61, 64).
Mr Creakle, cruel headmaster of Salem House school. 'I'll tell you what I am ... I'm a Tartar'. (Chapters 6, 7, 61).
Mrs Crupp, David's caretaker. 'Mr Copperfull ... I'm a mother myself'. (Chapters 23, 26, 28, 29, 34, 35, 37).

*E.M. Forster, *Aspects of the Novel*, p.79.

Rose Dartle, Mrs Steerforth's companion. 'She has sharpened her own face and figure these years past. She has worn herself away by constant sharpening. She is all edge.' Scarred physically by Steerforth, her behaviour also shows the marks of her passionate love for him. Her dark nature is tortured by frustration and hate. (Chapters 20, 24, 29, 32, 36, 46, 50, 56, 64).

Mr Dick, (Richard Babley). 'The most amenable and friendly creature in existence.' Simple-mindedness is almost a virtue as it allows him an honest, natural, and direct affection for everybody, especially Aunt Betsey and Doctor Strong. Spends his time writing a memoir, worrying about King Charles's head, and cheerfully flying kites. (Chapters 13, 14, 15, 17, 19, 34, 35, 38, 40, 42, 45, 49, 52, 62, 64).

Emily, Little Em'ly, Mr Peggotty's pretty niece, wants to be a lady even when she is a child, so her flight with Steerforth is no surprise. Quiet, and unsure of herself. (Chapters 3, 10, 21, 22, 30, 46, 50, 51, 55, 57, 63).

Martha Endell, Emily's friend and rescuer. (Chapters 22, 40, 46, 47, 50, 51, 57, 63).

Mrs Gummidge, Mr Peggotty's widowed housekeeper. 'I am a lone lorn creetur' . . . and everythink goes contrairy with me.' Always miserable, and saddened by memories of 'the old 'un', she changes greatly when Mr Peggotty's troubles start, and makes herself really useful to him. (Chapters 3, 10, 21, 22, 31, 32, 51, 57, 63).

Mrs Heep, Uriah's mother. (Chapters 17, 39, 52, etc).

Littimer, Steerforth's servant. 'His greatest claim to consideration was his respectability.' (Chapters 21, 22, 23, 28, 31, 32, 46, 61).

Mrs Markleham, Annie Strong's mother, 'the Old Soldier'. (Chapters 16, 19, 45, 64).

Jack Maldon, Annie Strong's 'needy and idle' cousin, suspected of having an affair with her. (Chapters 16, 19, 36, 42, 45, 64).

Emma Micawber, 'I never will desert Mr Micawber . . . There was a great deal of good in Mrs Micawber's heart.' A good wife and mother, despite 'pecuniary difficulties'. She is loyal and patient with her husband, whom she genuinely admires. She talks proudly of her 'family', but believes they and the world in general can't appreciate his talents. She is as sociable and hopeful (of 'something turning up') as he is, although, like him, her moods can change very quickly from joy to misery, and back. (Chapters 11, 12, 17, 27, 28, 36, 49, 52, 54, 57, 63).

Julia Mills, Dora's friend. 'A Voice from the Cloister . . . the Desert of Sahara.' Julia remembers her own misfortunes in love, and helps Dora and David. (Chapters 33, 37, 38, 41, 64).

Miss Mowcher, 'Ain't I volatile.' (see also notes on Serialisation.) (Chapters 22, 32, 61).

Mr Murdstone, David's stepfather, who spoils David's childhood with his gloomy and heartless cruelty. 'Mr Murdstone was firm; nobody in the world was to be as firm as Mr Murdstone; nobody else in his world was to be firm at all, for everybody was to be bent to his firmness.' (Chapters 2, 3, 4, 8, 9, 10, 14, 33, 59).

Jane Murdstone, Mr Murdstone's sister. 'Her firmness, and her strength of mind, and her common sense, and the whole diabolical catalogue of her unamiable qualities.' Very like her brother, she shows equally unpleasantly 'the gloomy taint that was in the Murdstone blood', and interferes both with David's love for his mother and in his relations with Dora. (Chapters 4, 8, 9, 10, 14, 26, 38, 59).

Mr Omer, tailor and undertaker. 'With the exception of my limbs and my breath, I am as hearty a man as can be.' (Chapters 9, 21, 30, 51).

Peggotty. 'The best, the truest, the most faithful, most devoted, and most self-denying friend and servant in the world, who had ever loved me dearly ... I felt towards her something I have never felt for any other human being.' Barkis's wife, and more of a friend than a servant to Clara Copperfield, Clara Peggotty remains to David as faithful and loving as a second mother, throughout his life. (Chapters 1–5, 8–10, 21, 30, 31, 33, 34, 37, 43, 51, 57, 59, 64).

Mr Peggotty. 'As good as gold and as true as steel.' Perfectly kind, generous, and open-hearted. Also very strong. His love for his niece Emily is powerful enough to make him forgive her and 'seek her through the wureld'. (Chapters 3, 7, 10, 21, 30, 31, 32, 40, 43, 46, 47, 50, 51, 55, 57, 63).

Ham Peggotty, Mr Peggotty's nephew. 'A huge, strong fellow of six feet high, broad in proportion, and round-shouldered, but with a simpering boy's face.' Brave, straightforward and kind, Ham becomes careless of his life after he loses Emily. (Chapters 1, 3, 7, 10, 21, 22, 30, 31, 32, 40, 51, 55).

Mr Spenlow, Dora's father and David's employer. 'I have a partner, Mr Jorkins.' (Chapters 23, 26, 29, 33, 35, 38).

Mrs Steerforth, Steerforth's proud mother. (Chapters 20, 24, 29, 32, 46, 56, 64).

Doctor Strong, David's headmaster at Canterbury, who later employs him as a secretary on his life's work, the Dictionary. Mild, kind, generous, and unworldly, he trusts his wife completely. (Chapters 16, 17, 19, 36, 42, 45, 64).

Annie Strong, the Doctor's pretty young wife. She is suspected of an affair with Jack Maldon, but is really loving and faithful to her husband. 'My love was founded on a rock, and it endures.' (Chapters 16, 17, 19, 36, 42, 45, 64).

Tommy Traddles. 'Traddles is a good fellow ... so much constancy and patience.' Cheerful, friendly, and good-natured at school, Traddles continues to be David's good friend in later life. He is sensible, reliable, and practical, and works hard and patiently to be able to fulfil his hopes of marrying his Sophy. Even after he is successful and very happily married, he continues his habit of drawing skeletons, and his unruly hair can still never be smoothed down. (Chapters 6, 7, 25, 27, 28, 34, 36, 38, 41, 43, 44, 49, 52, 54, 57, 59, 61, 64).

Mr Wickfield, Aunt Betsey's lawyer, Agnes's father. His weakness, fondness for wine, and excessive love for his daughter allow Uriah Heep to gain control over him and almost ruin him. He recovers his health and happiness when Heep is exposed. (Chapters 15, 16, 19, 35, 39, 42, 52, 54, 60).

Theme and unity

What is the novel *David Copperfield* about? The simplest answer, of course, is that it is about David Copperfield himself, and his development as a man. How does David develop? How does he change as the novel progresses?

Steerforth's servant Littimer once calls David 'young innocence' (Chapter 32). This name is appropriate. David is sensitive, honest, and loving as a child, and remains so all his life. He is also intelligent and observant, but he learns the harder facts of life very slowly. For example, it is clear from the first we see of Steerforth, when he 'takes care of' David's money, that Steerforth is not really as charming or good as he seems, or as David thinks he is. This becomes still clearer when he is so unpleasant to Mr Mell, and when we learn about Rosa Dartle. Even Agnes, who meets Steerforth only very briefly, sees through him at once and warns David about him. But David continues to trust and admire him, and introduces him to Mr Peggotty's household, which he ruins. Even after Steerforth runs off with Emily, David cannot quite think badly of his old friend. He is too innocent, trusting and thoughtless.

David also lacks firmness and self-discipline. His aunt, a good judge of character, is very well aware of this. David remembers how she 'hoped the life I was now to lead would make me firm and self-reliant, which was all I wanted' (Chapter 23). David also speaks of a similar 'distrust of myself, which has often beset me in life' (Chapter 19). This lack of firmness and self-reliance is made obvious on several occasions; for example, by the way David is cheated by servants and waiters. This happens to him very often, and almost constantly after he is married to Dora. He explains to her that 'These people turn out ill because we don't turn out very well ourselves' (Chapter 48).

David comes to realise that what is wrong is not just their incompetence with servants, and their general domestic difficulties. His whole marriage to Dora is a result of 'the first mistaken impulse of an undisciplined heart' (Chapter 45). He falls in love with Dora at first sight, before she even speaks, and before he has any idea of what sort of person she is. He thinks Dora is 'everything that everybody ever wanted' (Chapter 26), but when he explains his poverty to her he learns how unreasonable and unhelpful she can be. He ought to have remembered his other foolish young loves: Miss Shepherd, Miss Larkins, even little Em'ly and Rosa Dartle. But he goes ahead and marries Dora. Of course they are happy, but Dora is never quite a companion. David is almost lonely, and feels something is missing. He slowly realises that 'there can be no disparity in marriage like unsuitability of mind and purpose' (Chapter 45). Even silly Dora knows that they could not have remained happy together for very long. Her mind is too unlike David's.

After Dora dies, David begins to remember how many mistakes he has made. He realises that all his life it has made sense for him to be with Agnes, although he was too foolish—'blind, blind blind!' as his aunt said—to see this, and even failed to notice that Agnes loved him. He eventually realises that Agnes, and not Dora, is 'What I could have wished my wife to be' (Chapter 62). Agnes is not only beautiful and good, but close to him, 'suitable in mind and purpose', able to understand him wholly as a person, 'the centre of myself, the circle of my life' (Chapter 62). When he marries her, he feels complete, his life makes sense, and his happines is achieved.

David has already shown that he can be self-disciplined and resolute in some ways. When his aunt is ruined, he sets to work very hard indeed, with 'patient and continuous energy' (Chapter 42). The firmness and good sense he has to learn is not in his work, but in his personal relationships with other people. He has experienced firmness before, in his aunt's determined and independent way of life; and in the Murdstone's gloomy and loveless treatment of his mother. Dora is rather like Clara Copperfield (both are young, pretty, and foolish), and Aunt Betsey reminds David that in trying to 'form her mind' (Chapter 48), he must not repeat the cruelties of his stepfather, Murdstone. Firmness can be taken too far. Both David and his aunt learn, in the course of the novel, that love, generosity and trust must be mixed with discipline and self-control. Neither firmness, nor love, is enough entirely on its own.

David's two marriages are, of course, the major events of his personal life. Like many other novels of the nineteenth century, *David Copperfield* ends when its hero is happily married at last. But David's story is unusual: it ends with a second marriage, after we have learned all about the first. There are many other marriages in *David Copperfield*, too; the Micawbers, Murdstone's (twice), Doctor and Annie Strong, Barkis and Peggotty, Traddles and Sophy, Aunt Betsey's; even Mr Chillip's and Julia Mills's. His awareness of all these other relationships suggests to David—and perhaps to the reader, also—something about his own affairs. For example, it is when he hears Annie Strong talking to her husband that David first realises what might be wrong with his own marriage. David also learns, from seeing Traddles and Sophy together, how happy a marriage can be—and how different from his own marriage to Dora.

The question of love and marriage is a general and repeated concern, a theme, of *David Copperfield*. The very first words we hear David speak are ' "Peggotty . . . were you ever married?" ' She replies ' "Lord, Master Davy . . . What's put marriage in your head?" ' (Chapter 2). Whatever first puts marriage into David's head, it is a question that remains there long afterwards, and it is not properly answered until his final complete union with Agnes. Before this marriage to Agnes is possible, he must learn from his own early experience of his 'undisciplined heart', and from the many examples of loves and marriages he sees around him.

A criticism often made of *David Copperfield* is that parts of the novel are irrelevant, and have nothing to do with the main story of David's life. This is often said of the stories of Aunt Betsey and her husband, and of Doctor and Annie Strong. But such criticisms are unfair, because David learns from both experiences something more about the right way to be married, and how love between two people can work, or fail to work. Both stories add to his growing awareness. Once we recognise the importance of love and marriage in David's life, and as a theme in *David Copperfield*, the unity of the novel can be clearly seen. Each part of the story has its own function, and is carefully related to the other parts.

The simplest answer to the question 'What is *David Copperfield* about?' is the correct one. It is about David's development, and the lessons he has to learn before he can be completely happy. But these lessons are so often about finding the right way to love someone, and making the right marriage, that love and marriage themselves should be seen as part of the subject of the novel, part of what it is about. Agnes thinks that 'Simple love and truth will be strong in the end . . . real love and truth are stronger in the end than any evil or misfortune in the world'. Charles Dickens seems to have believed this too, and in writing *David Copperfield*, he tried to show how love can be real, and how it can be true.

Part 4

Hints for study

General

These notes, and other critical texts such as those suggested in Part 5, can help your study of *David Copperfield*, reminding you of the major parts of the story, of how it is told and of the nature and significance of the characters who appear in it. However, there is no substitute for a close, careful reading of the novel, making sure you understand it for yourself. The best way to improve your knowledge of *David Copperfield* is by reading it again, remembering all that you have learned the first time and seeing how you understood it as you did.

Usually the main problem with studying *David Copperfield* is not that it is difficult, or hard to understand, but that it is very long. The language is mostly quite simple, and David's story of himself is straightforward. But it is a long story, and full of significant details, which are sometimes not noticed, or forgotten. There are so many characters, too, that it is not always easy to remember the nature of each, or the part that each plays in the story.

How can these problems be overcome in your study of *David Copperfield*? The best answer is not to re-read the whole at once, but to concentrate on one aspect at a time and read only those parts of the novel that are relevant to it. We will consider first how this method applies to the study of character in *David Copperfield*.

Character

In answering examination questions, it is not usually good enough to state only what you know about a work of literature. You must also explain how you learned what you did, and why you think it is true. Ask yourself two questions about each character: not only 'What do we know about him or her?', but also 'How do we know it?'. Dickens presents characters to us carefully, and in many ways. Their appearances are described, and this very often tells us something about what they are like. We are told what they say and what other people say about them, and usually what David thinks about them, too. We also see their habits, and what they do. If you turn back to the list of characters in Part 3, you will find a brief description of each character, and a list of the chapters in which they appear. Take some of the characters, and look back at the chapters in which they are mentioned. Remind yourself of what each character is like, and see how we learn what we do about them. For example, you might reconsider Mr Murdstone, and look back at Chapters 2, 3, 4, 8, 9, 10, 14, 33, and 59. You need not read the whole of each chapter, only the bits which concern Murdstone. From these sections you should try to see how an opinion of Murdstone is formed: remembering the significance of his dark appearance; his cruelty to his wife, and to David; his relation to his sister; his conversation with Aunt Betsey, and so on. Notice how many views of him we are given: we learn what David thinks as a child, and as a grown man; we also know what Peggotty, Aunt Betsey, Mr Chillip, and even Mr Chillip's wife and neighbours (Chapter 59) think, too. And we learn a lot from what Mr Murdstone says himself: his warnings to his wife about firmness with David, for example. It is always useful to have a suitable quotation—something they say themselves, or something that is said about them—to illustrate and sum up a character. Several of these are included in the list in Part 3. Try to find more quotations of your own.

Look back at the characters, using the list in Part 3, until you are sure you know something about each of them, and can also say something about how you learned what you did. (There is also a selected list of chapters after each of the sketches of major characters in Part 3).

Theme and story

The same sort of method can be used in studying the story of *David Copperfield*. David's own story is central to the novel, and easily remembered. His development can be recalled by looking at some of the chapters from each section of it (see notes on Structure and Plot), perhaps the 'Retrospect' chapters (18, 43, 53, 64) and a few others. You should look again at the chapters in which each of the sub-plots reaches its crisis and resolution: Doctor Strong, Annie, and Jack Maldon (Chapter 45); Micawber, Heep, and Wickfield (Chapter 52); and Steerforth, Mr Peggotty and Emily (Chapters 50 and 55). In each case you should ask yourself what has led up to the events of these chapters, and, if necessary, trace the stories from their beginnings. For example, the Doctor Strong, Annie, and Jack Maldon story is continued in Chapters 16, 19, 36, 42, and 45. You should also consider how each story is related to David's own; for example, what does he learn from Doctor and Annie Strong, and how does he react to Steerforth?

David's relationship with Dora dominates his young life. It illustrates the theme of love and marriage which is central to *David Copperfield* as a whole. (See notes on Theme and Unity pp. 65-7). We see Dora and

David together in Chapters 26, 33, 37, 41, and 42. Their married life is shown in Chapters 43, 44, 48, and 53, and you should look at some of these chapters again, asking yourself questions such as How do David and Dora meet? What does he learn about her before marriage, and what after? Why does he love her? In what ways does he feel disappointed in her? What do other people, like his Aunt Betsey, or Agnes, or Dora's aunts, think about their marriage? What do we learn from *David Copperfield* about love and life in general?

Some general remarks

Always remember, as you read, to ask yourself both questions, both 'What?' and 'How?'. Not only *what* is going on, but *how* are we told about it. When you are studying character and story, notice also how these are presented. What sort of language does Dickens use? Consider, for example, all the varieties of direct speech—from Mr Micawber's to Mr Peggotty's. (Make sure that you have examples of each). How does Dickens describe a scene? (Details, significance, etc). How does he use humour? How does he use pathos? How does David tell his own story?

Most of these questions are partly answered in Part 3 of these notes, but you should ask and try to answer them for yourself, as you read. A good student of literature reads very thoroughly, and thinks carefully about the nature and meaning of what he reads.

To help you to think, here is a list of some typical questions about *David Copperfield*. The questions should help you to decide what to look for in going back over the novel. Try to answer each of them for yourself—at least make some notes—before you look at the outline answers. The questions are arranged roughly in increasing difficulty: the first six mostly test your knowledge and memory of the novel, the rest question more generally your understanding and appreciation of it.

Some possible questions

Here are some questions and brief suggestions about ways of answering them.

What was David's life like when he lived alone in London and worked at Murdstone and Grinby's?

Straightforward description: David's work in the warehouse; the people he met there; his wanderings alone in London; his poverty; what he ate; his meetings and life with the Micawbers; the King's Bench prison; his decision to run away (Chapters 11 and 12). Mention also his state of mind: he was sent away from home; an orphan alone in the world; great unhappiness and sense of desertion; the fanciful way he made stories of his experience (Chapter 11).

How does David react to the news that his aunt has lost all her money?

Like question 1, straightforward. See especially Chapters 34, 35, 36, 37. Your answer should note both David's actions—his arrangements with Traddles, Spenlow, and Doctor Strong—but also his mood and thoughts—great determination, enthusiasm, etc. Note particularly how it affects his relationship with Dora, and what he thinks about this (Chapter 37).

Write brief notes on the characters of each of the following: Clara Peggotty; Jane Murdstone; Littimer; Mrs Gummidge; Mr Wickfield; Mr Dick; Uriah Heep; Mrs Micawber; Mr Peggotty.

See pp.60 & 63-5.

Compare and contrast the characters of Agnes and Dora.

See notes on Agnes; but first look back at some of the chapters in which each character appears, and note how they are alike, and how different. Note particularly Chapters 42 and 53, in which they appear together.

Choose one character from *David Copperfield* who develops in the course of the novel, and show how he or she changes.

Betsey Trotwood and David himself are the two best examples of characters who develop in the novel. (See notes on Betsey Trotwood, and Theme and Unity.) You might write an answer on either of them, showing the changes which occur in their thought and behaviour, and what causes these. A neat (and simpler) way of answering this question would be to explain the development of a minor character. For example, when Mrs Gummidge sees Mr Peggotty's sorrow, she changes from an idle, self-pitying 'lone lorn creetur' ' (Chapter 3), into a useful member of Mr Peggotty's household (Chapters 31 and 32, etc.)

Describe one character in *David Copperfield* whose appearance or manner tells us something significant about them.

See Part 3, notes on Description, Realism, and Imagination; and on Character. Micawber and Murdstone are the examples used, but you could very well discuss Uriah Heep, Traddles, or several others.

Which events in David's life do you think affected him most?

You might think about David being sent away from home; his experiences at his schools; his mother's death; his time working alone in London; his running away to his aunt; her financial ruin; his two marriages; or several other events. Discuss the effect each of these happenings had upon him ; why they were important to him; what he thought about them and what he learned from them; how they helped him to grow up and to develop into the man he has become at the time he writes.

Choose one incident from *David Copperfield* that you found amusing, and say why you thought it was funny.

There are many funny incidents in *David Copperfield*: you should choose the one you can discuss best. You might, for example, choose the scene when David and Traddles go to visit Dora's aunts (Chapter 41), and suggest in what ways it is amusing. Situation, personality and dialogue all add to the effect. David looks back with humour on his difficult position and his nervousness about it. He describes with wit and irony the strange old aunts and their odd way of sharing the conversation between them.

You might use the same method to talk about Traddles's visit to David and Dora's for dinner (Chapter 44), or about a number of other scenes. In any case make sure you choose a scene you understand and can write about thoroughly.

Dora and David have a lot of trouble with their housekeeping. Why does this happen, and why does it make them particularly unhappy?

Dora is a very bad housekeeper. She is unhappy because David scolds her or tries to reason with her. David is unhappy not just about the housekeeping, but because his attempts to talk to and teach Dora fail. From these failures, he comes to realise her limitations, and that their marriage is not perfect.

That is a very simple answer, and needs support from Chapters 44, 48, and 53.

What might David learn from Traddles's marriage to Sophy?

See notes on Theme and Unity, and look at Chapters 27, 41, 59, 61, 62, and 64.

Give an account of David's relationship with Agnes, up to their marriage in Chapter 62.

The point is that Agnes always loves David, and in a way he always loves her, but he does not realise this properly, or tell the reader directly, until Chapters 58, 60, and 62. Until then, he thinks they have a sort of brother and sister relationship. The way he depends on her is mentioned in most of the chapters in which Agnes appears. There are also many hints about David's true feelings, for example in Chapters 34, 35 and 39.

Dickens's characters are often said to be unrealistic, or caricatures. Do you think this criticism is useful in discussing *David Copperfield*?

See notes on Character. Notice that the criticism suggests something about Dickens's method, so it can be useful without being entirely correct. Your answer will depend on what you think of Dickens's characters, and you should illustrate and support your views fully by discussing several characters in *David Copperfield*.

Some critics find it unconvincing that Steerforth and Emily run away together. Do you think that we ought to be surprised that they do?

See notes on Steerforth and Emily. This question concerns not only the characters of Steerforth and Emily, but the way *David Copperfield* is written. (See notes on A Novel of Personal Memory.) In telling the story and creating his characters, Dickens gives many hints of what will happen latter. We can see that Steerforth is not as fine and honest as David thought (Chapters 6 and 7). His charm is an act (Chapter 21). We know what he might think about Emily (Chapters 6 and 21). We know that Emily always wanted to be a lady (Chapter 3), and what she might think of Steerforth (Chapter 10, 21, and 30). So although her flight is a shock, it is one that we have been prepared for, and that follows from what has gone before.

How is childhood and upbringing treated in David Copperfield?

Think of all the parents who appear in *David Copperfield*: the mothers of Steerforth, Uriah Heep, and Annie Strong; Mr Spenlow, Mr Wickfield, and Mr Peggotty (really like a father to Ham and little Em'ly). David himself has several parent-figures: his own mother, of course, and his stepfather Murdstone, and, later, Peggotty and Aunt Betsey become like second mothers to him. ('My poor mother herself could not have loved me better' Chapter 37). We see nearly as many parent-child relationships as we do marriages. (Sometimes the two are almost confused, as in Doctor Strong's marriage to Annie, Chapter 45.) There are also very many orphans, or children with only one parent, in *David Copperfield*. The problems of childhood and upbringing appear so often that they might also be called a theme of *David Copperfield*.

In answering this question, you might discuss several examples of the way childhood and parents can affect later life: for example, the way Steerforth and perhaps Dora and even little Em'ly are spoiled by over-loving parents, or the way Mr Wickfield loves Agnes. You should of course also consider David's own childhood, and the influences on him of his mother; Murdstone; Peggotty; and Aunt Betsey; and of his various adventures as a boy, at school and in London.

Part 5

Suggestions for further reading

The text

The text used in writing these notes is the Penguin edition of *David Copperfield,* Penguin Books, Harmondsworth, 1966, which is based on the single-volume edition of 1850, with some corrections from the last edition published in Dickens's lifetime. The Penguin edition modernises some spelling and punctuation. Since there are so many modern editions of *David Copperfield*, with differently numbered pages, references throughout these notes are to chapters, not pages.

Other works by Charles Dickens

Charles Dickens was a man of great creative energy, and published fourteen novels during his lifetime: *Pickwick Papers* (1837), *Oliver Twist* (1837), *Nicholas Nickleby* (1839), *The Old Curiosity Shop* (1841), *Barnaby Rudge* (1841), *Martin Chuzzlewit* (1844), *Dombey and Son* (1848), *David Copperfield* (1850), *Bleak House* (1853), *Hard Times* (1854), *Little Dorrit* (1857), *A Tale of Two Cities* (1859), *Great Expectations* (1861), *Our Mutual Friend* (1865). He was at work on a fifteenth novel, *Edwin Drood*, when he died in 1870. Most of his novels are available in cheap modern editions.

Biographies and critical studies can be helpful, but one of the best ways to learn more about an author is to read more of what he wrote himself. Dickens's first novels, *Pickwick Papers* and *Oliver Twist*, are entertaining and easily read. But the best one to read in studying *David Copperfield* is *Great Expectations*. It is a very fine novel in itself, and can be interestingly compared with *David Copperfield. Great Expectations*, like *David Copperfield*, is written in the first person, and is the hero's recollection of his own life.

In addition to his novel writing, Dickens was an energetic journalist, and an enthuastic correspondent: there are three large volumes of his collected letters. (Charles Dickens, *The Letters of Charles Dickens* ed. Walter Dexter, (3 vols), the Nonesuch Press, London, 1938). As a popular and committed public figure, Dickens also made many speeches, and these have been collected in one volume. (Charles Dickens, *The Speeches of Charles Dickens*, ed. K.J. Fielding, Oxford University Press, Oxford, 1960.)

General reading

Biographical
There are many biographies of Charles Dickens: the two best and most famous are,

FORSTER, JOHN, *The Life of Charles Dickens*, ED. J.W.T. LEY: Palmer, London, 1928. This is a personal memory of Dickens by one of his closest friends and advisers. Ley's edition includes further details that Forster left out. It is a very long work: Books I and VI are most useful in studying *David Copperfield*.

JOHNSON, EDGAR: *Charles Dickens: His Tragedy and Triumph*, Gollancz, London, 1953. A modern and very thorough biography. Also long; Parts One and Seven are most relevant to *David Copperfield*.

Critical Studies

BUTT, JOHN, AND TILLOTSON, KATHLEEN: *Dickens at Work*, Methuen, London, 1957. Chapter 6 explains how Dickens planned and wrote *David Copperfield* in serial form.

COLLINS, PHILIP: *Charles Dickens: David Copperfield*, Arnold, London, 1977. An excellent brief introduction to the novel, simple and clear.

FIELDING, K.J.: *Charles Dickens: A Critical Introduction*, Longmans, London, 1958. A simple account of Dickens's career as an author. There is a chapter on *David Copperfield*.

HOUSE, HUMPHRY: *The Dickens World*, Oxford University Press, London, 1941. Interesting on Dickens and his society, the historical background to the novels.

LEAVIS, F.R., AND LEAVIS, Q.D.: *Dickens the Novelist*, Chatto and Windus, London, 1970. Contains a good chapter on *David Copperfield*.

MILLER, J. HILLIS: *Charles Dickens: The World of his Novels*, Oxford University Press, London, 1958. A very interesting chapter on *David Copperfield*.

MONOD, SYLVERE: *Dickens the Novelist*, University of Oklahoma Press, Oklahoma, 1968. One of the longest and most thorough critical discussions of *David Copperfield*.

NEEDHAM, GWENDOLYN: 'The Undisciplined Heart of David Copperfield' in *Nineteenth Century Fiction*, IX, September, 1954, p.81–107. An excellent essay on David's development.

ORWELL, GEORGE: 'Charles Dickens', in *Collected Essays*, Secker and Warburg, London 1961. A good general essay on Dickens.

WALL, STEPHEN, (ED.): *Charles Dickens* (Penguin Critical Anthologies), Penguin Books, Harmondsworth, 1970. A collection of short critical statements on Dickens, including several about *David Copperfield*.

WILSON, ANGUS: *The World of Charles Dickens*, Secker and Warburg, London, 1970. Has many excellent illustrations, which help to give an idea of what life was like in Dickens's times.

The author of these notes

RANDALL STEVENSON was educated at the University of Edinburgh, where he won the James Elliot Prize. After a year teaching in a training college in North-West State, Nigeria, and two years as a research student in the University of Oxford, he returned to Edinburgh University where he has been a lecturer in English literature since 1978. Co-author with Colin Nicholson of York Notes on *The Sound and the Fury* and on *The Crying of Lot 49*, he has also written several articles on twentieth-century fiction and drama, and reviews theatre regularly for BBC radio and for *Times Literary Supplement*. His study of recent fiction, *The British Novel since the Thirties*, will be published in 1986.

York Notes: list of titles

CHINUA ACHEBE
Things Fall Apart
EDWARD ALBEE
Who's Afraid of Virginia Woolf?
ANONYMOUS
Beowulf
Everyman
W. H. AUDEN
Selected Poems
JANE AUSTEN
Emma
Mansfield Park
Northanger Abbey
Persuasion
Pride and Prejudice
Sense and Sensibility
SAMUEL BECKETT
Waiting for Godot
ARNOLD BENNETT
The Card
JOHN BETJEMAN
Selected Poems
WILLIAM BLAKE
Songs of Innocence, Songs of Experience
ROBERT BOLT
A Man For All Seasons
HAROLD BRIGHOUSE
Hobson's Choice
ANNE BRONTË
The Tenant of Wildfell Hall
CHARLOTTE BRONTË
Jane Eyre
EMILY BRONTË
Wuthering Heights
ROBERT BROWNING
Men and Women
JOHN BUCHAN
The Thirty-Nine Steps
JOHN BUNYAN
The Pilgrim's Progress
BYRON
Selected Poems
GEOFFREY CHAUCER
Prologue to the Canterbury Tales
The Clerk's Tale
The Franklin's Tale
The Knight's Tale
The Merchant's Tale
The Miller's Tale
The Nun's Priest's Tale

The Pardoner's Tale
The Wife of Bath's Tale
Troilus and Criseyde
SAMUEL TAYLOR COLERIDGE
Selected Poems
SIR ARTHUR CONAN DOYLE
The Hound of the Baskervilles
WILLIAM CONGREVE
The Way of the World
JOSEPH CONRAD
Heart of Darkness
STEPHEN CRANE
The Red Badge of Courage
BRUCE DAWE
Selected Poems
DANIEL DEFOE
Moll Flanders
Robinson Crusoe
WALTER DE LA MARE
Selected Poems
SHELAGH DELANEY
A Taste of Honey
CHARLES DICKENS
A Tale of Two Cities
Bleak House
David Copperfield
Great Expectations
Hard Times
Oliver Twist
The Pickwick Papers
EMILY DICKINSON
Selected Poems
JOHN DONNE
Selected Poems
GERALD DURRELL
My Family and Other Animals
GEORGE ELIOT
Middlemarch
Silas Marner
The Mill on the Floss
T. S. ELIOT
Four Quartets
Murder in the Cathedral
Selected Poems
The Cocktail Party
The Waste Land
J. G. FARRELL
The Siege of Krishnapur
WILLIAM FAULKNER
The Sound and the Fury

HENRY FIELDING
Joseph Andrews
Tom Jones
F. SCOTT FITZGERALD
Tender is the Night
The Great Gatsby
GUSTAVE FLAUBERT
Madame Bovary
E. M. FORSTER
A Passage to India
Howards End
JOHN FOWLES
The French Lieutenant's Woman
JOHN GALSWORTHY
Strife
MRS GASKELL
North and South
WILLIAM GOLDING
Lord of the Flies
The Spire
OLIVER GOLDSMITH
She Stoops to Conquer
The Vicar of Wakefield
ROBERT GRAVES
Goodbye to All That
GRAHAM GREENE
Brighton Rock
The Heart of the Matter
The Power and the Glory
WILLIS HALL
The Long and the Short and the Tall
THOMAS HARDY
Far from the Madding Crowd
Jude the Obscure
Selected Poems
Tess of the D'Urbervilles
The Mayor of Casterbridge
The Return of the Native
The Woodlanders
L. P. HARTLEY
The Go-Between
NATHANIEL HAWTHORNE
The Scarlet Letter
SEAMUS HEANEY
Selected Poems
ERNEST HEMINGWAY
A Farewell to Arms
The Old Man and the Sea
SUSAN HILL
I'm the King of the Castle
BARRY HINES
Kes
HOMER
The Iliad
The Odyssey

GERARD MANLEY HOPKINS
Selected Poems
TED HUGHES
Selected Poems
ALDOUS HUXLEY
Brave New World
HENRIK IBSEN
A Doll's House
HENRY JAMES
The Portrait of a Lady
Washington Square
BEN JONSON
The Alchemist
Volpone
JAMES JOYCE
A Portrait of the Artist as a Young Man
Dubliners
JOHN KEATS
Selected Poems
PHILIP LARKIN
Selected Poems
D. H. LAWRENCE
Selected Short Stories
Sons and Lovers
The Rainbow
Women in Love
HARPER LEE
To Kill a Mocking-Bird
LAURIE LEE
Cider with Rosie
CHRISTOPHER MARLOWE
Doctor Faustus
HERMAN MELVILLE
Moby Dick
THOMAS MIDDLETON *and*
WILLIAM ROWLEY
The Changeling
ARTHUR MILLER
A View from the Bridge
Death of a Salesman
The Crucible
JOHN MILTON
Paradise Lost I & II
Paradise Lost IV & IX
Selected Poems
V. S. NAIPAUL
A House for Mr Biswas
ROBERT O'BRIEN
Z for Zachariah
SEAN O'CASEY
Juno and the Paycock
GEORGE ORWELL
Animal Farm
Nineteen Eighty-four